# PUTTING TEENS FIRST IN LIBRARY SERVICES

## A ROAD MAP

### EDITED BY LINDA W. BRAUN AND SHANNON PETERSON

**YALSA**
Young Adult Library Services Association
A Division of the American Library Association

ISBN: 9780838989616


Library of Congress Cataloging-in-Publication Data

Names: Braun, Linda W., editor. | Peterson, Shannon, editor.
Title: Putting teens first in library services : a road map /
editors, Linda W. Braun, Shannon Peterson.
Description: Chicago : Young Adult Library Services Association
(YALSA), a division of the American Library Association
(ALA), [2017] | Includes bibliographical references.
Identifiers: LCCN 2017022060 | ISBN 9780838989616 (paperback)
Subjects: LCSH: Young adults' libraries—United States—
Administration. | Libraries and teenagers—United States. |
Young adults' libraries—United States—Case studies. |
Libraries and teenagers—United States—Case studies.
Classification: LCC Z718.5 .P88 2017 | DDC 027.62/6—dc23 LC
record available at https://lccn.loc.gov/2017022060

The paper used in this publication meets the requirements of
ANSI/NISO Z39.48-1992 (Permanence of Paper). ∞

Printed in the United States of America

21 20 19 18 17    5 4 3 2 1

# Contents

**List of Figures** ......................................................................................iii

**Acknowledgments** ..................................................................................v

**Introduction,** Maureen Hartman ..................................................... 1

YALSA Case Study
Teen Tech Squad ..................................................................................5

YALSA Case Study
Implementing Connected Learning and Twenty-First-Century Skill
Development in Programming..............................................................8

CHAPTER 1
**Continuous Learning,** Megan Christine-Carlin Burton..................11

YALSA Case Study
Kentucky Youth Film Festival .............................................................38

YALSA Case Study
Connecting with Teens through Personal Interests ...........................41

CHAPTER 2
**Supporting Youth Learning,** Crystle Martin ................................44

YALSA Case Study
Digital Storytelling.................................................................63

YALSA Case Study
A New Vision for a New Teen Space ......................................66

CHAPTER 3
**Working Together: Youth-Adult Partnerships to Enhance**
**Youth Voice,** Juan Rubio ....................................................69

YALSA Case Study
IDEA Lab Tech Team Internship ...........................................96

CHAPTER 4
**Engaging with Community,** Jessi Snow, with contributions
by Shannon Peterson.............................................................99

YALSA Case Study
Summer Teen Interns........................................................... 127

CHAPTER 5
**Assessments and Outcome-Based Evaluation in Formal**
**and Informal Learning Spaces,** Amanda Waugh, Natalie
Greene Taylor, and Kelly Hoffman .......................................131

# Appendices

APPENDIX A
The Future of Library Services for and with Teens: A Call to
Action Executive Summary ................................................. 165

APPENDIX B
Teens First Infographic ...................................................... 170

APPENDIX C
Core Professional Values for the Teen Services Profession................171

**About the Authors and Editors** ................................................. 179

# List of Figures

## Chapter 1

Figure 1-1. Learning Organization Checklist ..................................... 15

Figure 1-2. IMLS 21st-Century Skills Assessment Framework ......... 16

Figure 1-3. Professional Development Planning Checklist .............. 17

## Chapter 2

Figure 2-1. Tips on Bringing Connected Learning to Libraries ........ 51

## Chapter 3

Figure 3-1. Case 1: The Case of the Missing Pages—Helping
Students Move Forward ................................................................... 72

Figure 3-2. Icebreakers .................................................................... 82

Figure 3-3. Building Relationships and Merging Adult-Youth
Domains ........................................................................................... 86

Figure 3-4. Building Relationships: Merged Adult-Youth
Domains ........................................................................................... 86

Figure 3-5. Case 2: The Case of the Evil Agents—Identifying Moments in Which Youth Feel Heard ................................................. 88

Figure 3-6. Case 3: Ice Cream and Ketchup .................................... 91

# Chapter 4

Figure 4-1. The Spectrum of Community Engagement ................... 103

Figure 4-2. The Implicit Association Test ....................................... 110

Figure 4-3. Care about Community .................................................. 111

Figure 4-4. What Is the Asset-Based Community Development Model? ................................................................................................. 115

Figure 4-5. Case Study: Leadership Anchorage Leads to Collective Impact ................................................................................ 119

Figure 4-6. Five Elements of Collective Impact .............................. 121

# Chapter 5

Figure 5-1. Case Study: Observations from a School Library Administrator ..................................................................................... 136

Figure 5-2. Data-Gathering Techniques ......................................... 139

Figure 5-3. Case Study: Focus Groups in an Informal Learning Space ................................................................................... 145

Figure 5-4. YOUmedia ..................................................................... 147

Figure 5-5. Case Study: Providence Public Library's Teen Squad .................................................................................................. 151

Figure 5-6. Case Study: Digital Artifacts ....................................... 156

Figure 5-7. Assessment Resources .................................................. 160

# Acknowledgments

The editors wish to thank the authors of YALSA's "The Future of Library Services for and with Teens: A Call to Action"—Linda W. Braun, Maureen Hartman, Sandra Hughes-Hassell, and Kafi Kumasi—for synthesizing and articulating the direction that teen library services must take. They also thank the Institute of Museum and Library Services for supporting that early vision as well as YALSA Executive Director Beth Yoke for engaging the teen services community in moving it forward.

# Introduction

## MAUREEN HARTMAN

The future of library services for teens is not far off in the distance; it is here. Even before the 2014 publication of YALSA's *The Future of Library Services for and with Teens: A Call to Action* (referred to as the *Futures Report*), library leaders and staff working directly with teens were exploring ideas and initiating new services and programs. This helped ensure that library services for and with teens remain critical, particularly as the needs of youth—and their communities—continue to evolve.

If libraries neglect the evolution of their teen library services for and with teens, or neglect the role of library staff members in implementing these services, they risk a future in which libraries themselves are no longer valuable to community stakeholders, potential advocates, or even young people.

The *Futures Report* summarizes data and evidence related to the changing demographics, reality, and needs of teens ages 12–18. The report was the end product of a yearlong study funded by the Institute of Museum and Library Services (IMLS) that brought together library staff and youth development stakeholders and provided opportunities for members of these groups to discuss key issues in the lives of teens and in out-of-school-time services.

The *Futures Report* notes that there are over 40 million adolescents in the United States today, and, based on research from the Pew Research Center's Internet and American Life Project, these teens are using libraries. Demographics for the age group are shifting: 46% are children of color, and more than one-fifth are immigrants or children of immigrants. More than 3 million young people drop out of school every year, and teens are entering the workforce without the skills they will need to be successful.

This data, as well as the exponential growth in the use of technology, points to a paradigm shift in library services for and with teens. As key institutions within communities, libraries must shift thinking about how to deliver services to teens in order to meet their evolving needs.

The *Futures Report* proposes a vision for library teen services. It also outlines five areas that libraries need to focus on in order to make this vision a reality:

- Embrace teen library staff's role as facilitators rather than experts.

- Embrace new roles and measurements of success.

- Partner strategically to reach beyond the library's walls.

- Create a whole-library and whole-school approach to serving teens in physical spaces and online.

- Support library staff in gaining new skills.

The challenges of achieving these goals are real and will take time and commitment at a variety of levels. The perspectives that follow in this volume provide background information and new ways to think about some of the issues and ideas explored in the *Futures Report*. As a result, this book—based on research and practical ideas and advice from experts and practitioners in the field—is a guide and foundation for teen library services. While the advice contained herein is likely most beneficial to library staff who work directly with teens, it is also helpful to administrators and other advocates and leaders in setting both a research and practical framework for the specific cultural changes that libraries need to undertake.

Library staff are the key facilitators in successfully delivering services to teens now and in the future. In her chapter, "Continuous Learning," Megan Christine-Carlin Burton outlines the components that library staff at all levels need to add to their skills in order to support a successful evolution of services. Particularly compelling is her identification of the *Futures Report* as a call to action for "library leadership at all levels" to develop both their own future-ready learning and development plans as well as organization-wide plans for all staff in a library. Burton highlights strategies like "innovation time," badging, and learning playlists as avenues for library staff to consider in furthering their own continuous learning.

In "Supporting Youth Learning," Crystle Martin reminds us that learning and fun aren't oppositional—fun should be embedded in every opportunity; however, no library service or program can be "just about fun." Program designers should think about how to add elements of problem solving, thinking, and collaboration into the design of their programs for teens. While the connected learning framework for education may not be new to readers of this book, a reminder of the three spheres of connected learning—peer-supported, interest-based, and academic-oriented—is important. Framing academic work as "future" can better help library staff envision the role they might have—and already do have—in supporting young people in making connections between the things they are learning (and enjoying) and how they might apply those skills in the future.

Youth voice, long an underlying value in teen library services, is tackled in a more nuanced, deep way by Juan Rubio in "Working Together: Youth-Adult Partnerships to Enhance Youth Voice." Rubio provides additional ways to think about the balance that adults who work with teens manage on a daily basis, by recognizing:

- Teens' own power and voice and not overstepping their role as an adult in the experience.

- Ways to better understand the critical importance of the adults' role in a learning space.

- The importance of making room for young people by posing questions, keeping momentum moving, and staying in partnership together.

We've all seen adults who dominate, forgetting to leave space for youth voice, or the opposite, those who abandon their role, leaving youth frustrated in their learning. Rubio reminds us about the important role of amplification that adults can play in a society that does not hold youth voice equal to that of other more privileged groups.

Jessi Snow's "Engaging with Community" looks at another important area of growth that libraries will need to strengthen services for teens. Snow defines what community engagement is, makes a case for the value of this focus for libraries, and provides a series of steps for managing a community-engagement process. Throughout the chapter, the author includes thought-provoking ideas for library staff to consider as they work to strengthen their library's capacity to partner strategically with others on behalf of teens in their community.

"Assessments and Outcome-Based Evaluation in Formal and Informal Learning Spaces" by Amanda Waugh, Natalie Greene Taylor, and Kelly Hoffman provides strong background and justification for the importance of outcome-based measures. Even more compelling to practitioners are the extremely valuable (and worthy of framing in offices) list of ways to evaluate—including surveys, observations, pre-/post-tests, and portfolios. Many library staff are most familiar with surveys, and yet there are so many other ways to undertake assessment.

The future of library services for and with teens is about learning: supporting young people in their learning journeys as well as enhancing their existing skills and furthering the development of library staff. The ideas presented here give all those working with and for teens in and through libraries a very good place to start.

## Notes

1. Linda W. Braun, Maureen Hartman, Sandra Hughes-Hassell, and Kafi Kumasi, *The Future of Library Services for and with Teens: A Call to Action* (IMLS and YALSA, January 2014), http://www.ala.org/yaforum/sites/ala.org.yaforum/files/content/YALSA_nationalforum_final.pdf (accessed February 21, 2017); Kathryn Zickuhr and Lee Rainie, *Younger Americans and Public Libraries* (Pew Research Center, September 10, 2014), http://www.pewinternet.org/2014/09/10/younger-americans-and-public-libraries/ (accessed February 21, 2017).

2. Braun et al., *Future of Library Services*.

## HENNEPIN COUNTY LIBRARY (MN)

# Teen Tech Squad

### KATHERINE DEBERTIN

## What Did You Want to Achieve?

At the Hennepin County Library we set out to offer persistent programming opportunities for youth to increase their ability to express themselves using technology, and to explore and engage in connected learning with their peers. With the Teen Tech Squad we also wanted to provide meaningful employment opportunities for older teens to increase their leadership skills (including communication, problem solving, and resilience) as they prepare for their post-secondary pursuits.

## Overview of the Program/Project

Hennepin County Library's Teen Tech Squad program currently employs 30 teens across seven branch tech squads. The teens research, design, and lead interactive experiences for youth who learn STEAM skills through tinkering and making. While each squad has taken a slightly different focus for their community, workshops range from making bubblegum to creating cities out of cardboard, and from recording and mixing music to 3D modeling and printing. Participants and teen leaders alike create original digital and artistic content and innovate in supportive and flexible programming after school and on the weekends.

## What Challenges Did You Face and How Did You Overcome Them?

Growing and clarifying our internal systems of support (from human resources, to IT support, to learning and development needs for staff) alongside this new model of programming has been the biggest challenge in building and sustaining this work. For example, the role of the librarians who facilitate tech squads has shifted to include more management and supervisory tasks while the job classification (and associated access to training, and management conversations) has not evolved at the same pace. Additionally, more staff and supervisors (not just the youth services librarians!) are involved in supervising, leading, evaluating, and supporting this work than in the past. Creating clear expectations, roles, and paths for communication has been essential to growing our capacity as an organization.

## What Did You Learn?

We have long known that you can't wait for an idea to be fully baked before getting started—but we learned that it takes a whole-library approach (and teen voice and leadership) to build, sustain, and integrate this model of programming into the way we make programming decisions, delegate responsibilities, and reframe our definitions of expectations and success. We are continuously learning how to talk about trying something new, taking risks, and learning in public as we grow new roles for our staff.

## How Does This Work Connect to YALSA's Futures Report and Vision?

This project intersects with envisioned definitions of literacy, with the learning ecosystem for youth today, with the importance of connected learning, and opportunities to learn in different ways. However, the area of the *Futures Report* that resonates most with this project has to do with how we shift our mindset to grow with our young people. As the *Futures Report* states:

> In a society in which some young people are succeeding and others are being left behind, libraries play a critical role in preparing ALL teens to be productive, engaged citizens in both their work and personal lives. For libraries to make this needed shift, however, five fundamental elements must change, including:
>
> 1. Embracing our role as facilitator rather than expert.
>
> 2. Refocusing beyond our traditional roles and traditional measurements of success
>
> 3. Partnering strategically to reach beyond the library's walls
>
> 4. Creating a whole-library and whole-school approach to serving teens in physical spaces and online
>
> 5. Supporting library staff in gaining new skills.

Our teen tech squad work brings all of these to life in our libraries.

# Implementing Connected Learning and Twenty-First-Century Skill Development in Programming

ADRIENNE STROCK

## What Did You Want to Achieve?

At Nashville Public Library, staff are being intentional about incorporating connected learning and the development of twenty-first-century skills into program planning and design. This is important so we can offer teens leadership opportunities, take their interests to heart when planning programs, become more production-centered, and help them grow into adults who will be successful in life.

## Overview of the Program/Project

I led staff through an all-day professional development training that focused on many of the concepts outlined in the Futures Report such as connected learning, mentoring, HOMAGO (Hanging Out, Messing Around, Geeking Out), and twenty-first-century skill development. During this training, I introduced staff to the program planning and reflection sheets I had developed. I followed up with staff as necessary to ensure they understood and were applying the concepts to program design.

## What Challenges Did You Face and How Did You Overcome Them?

I think that the greatest challenge was introducing the concepts to a brand-new team of staff and facilitating a shift into planning programs that are designed around specific outcomes. Staff submit monthly program planning and reflection sheets so that they can be intentional in the design and planning of programs. The sheets also demonstrate how deeply staff understand the concepts and how well they are applying the concepts to program design.

## What Did You Learn?

If staff are excited about the evolution of teen services in libraries, then there are more opportunities to think differently about what programming can look like in twenty-first-century libraries. Staff went through growing pains but are committed to learning to adapt programs based on teen interests and to develop production-centered activities that engage teens.

## How Does This Work Connect to YALSA's Futures Report and Vision?

Twenty-first-century skill development and connected learning are at the core of the Nashville Public Library's Main Library Teen Center. Staff have embraced the concepts and continue to work with teens to design programs that draw teens to them.

Nina NeSmith, a Teen Services Specialist at the Library, stated it this way:

"The application of twenty-first-century skill development is very helpful in allowing me to have a goal for what I want teens to take out of programming. I am able to identify soft skills that teens need to develop in adulthood, thus developing skills for job readiness and life. For instance, in the program I created and facilitated in the fall called Mission Makeover, I focused on skills essential in professional development and job readiness like dress and grooming, how to create a résumé, and proper interview etiquette. It also presented the perfect opportunity to

incorporate connected learning principles so that the teens had tangible products that could be used in both the present and future. Teens were able to choose interview attire from a 'boutique' created through donations from library staff and peers. They even got to model their ensembles in a fashion show. The teens also created résumés, made soaps, and created 'professional' hairstyles throughout the program series. Using twenty-first-century skills along with a sprinkling of connected learning is an awesome recipe for creating quality programming for the teens we serve.

# CHAPTER 1
# Continuous Learning

MEGAN CHRISTINE-CARLIN BURTON

## Introduction

YALSA's *The Future of Library Services for and with Teens: A Call to Action* makes it clear: Teens are an important part of library services, their needs are changing, and the way libraries support teens is also changing. In 2016 the U.S. Census Bureau estimated that 41 million adolescents ages 10–19 live in the United States—13% of the total American population.[1] Add to that a dramatic shift in ethnic and racial diversity—an increase of 46%—between the two most recent Census Reports. Although some positive economic developments for families with unemployed members have come about with the creation of nearly 13 million jobs since the end of the recession,[2] teens are increasingly entering the workforce unprepared.[3] Teens without marketable skills, evidence-based credentials, résumé-building experience, or enough education encounter barriers to entry-level jobs.[4] The "opportunity gap" is widening, and disparate communities have visibly different access to the technology and training that will provide teens with a competitive edge in their career paths.[5] Closing this gap requires libraries to do much more than add emerging technologies to their array of tools and services: the current climate of teen services demands that library staff at all levels be willing to make greater changes in how and what they do for teens. In some instances, these changes will require that library staff challenge themselves to never stop learning.

# Never Stop Learning

Imagine the information landscape of the future. Ask yourself:

- What learning is taking place in this future information world, and what do learning institutions look like?

- How are libraries supporting formal and informal learning opportunities across the landscape?

- What role does the library play in the new learning ecology, and what are our roles as facilitators in that cycle?

Consider the communities of people connecting and learning in the future information world. We have entered a new era of learning in the library, both when it comes to library staff's own professional development and the learning needs of library patrons. At the center of the vision we are working toward as library professionals in public and school settings is support of lifelong learning, including lifelong library staff learning.

Learning is a continuous project that we are all working on each day, and within this project it is important to stay agile with one's own learning goals. Rather than having a working understanding of many areas of need, there is a risk of competency in only one area of expertise, which can potentially cause skill atrophy.

In 2013 the Young Adult Library Services Association's (YALSA) National Forum on Libraries and Teens surveyed the current needs of teens and synthesized their findings in a report titled *The Future of Library Services for and with Teens: A Call to Action*, frequently referred to as the *Futures Report*.[6] The envisioned future of library services places teens at the center of library services, program implementation, and delivery. Teens are in need of services and programs that place youth voice at the center and that value teens' unique role in society as the next electorate, decision makers, and lifelong learners.

Professional development that prepares library staff for this teen-centered future of library services needs to take a holistic view of services and community needs. For this to occur, the *Futures Report* guidelines must become part of all staff development, regardless of service area or specific focus. Ultimately, the report is a learning tool for both individual and group learning in the current teen library service landscape.

Along with the *Futures Report*'s call to action, guidelines for advocating for more staff dialogue on training to meet the needs of teens can be found in "The Importance of a Whole Library Approach to Public Library Young Adult Services: A YALSA Issue Paper." One critical takeaway from this document is that all staff have the responsibility to collaborate when it comes to supporting teen and overall community needs. "It is crucial that all library staff have the skills and knowledge necessary to serve the young adult population with respect and first-rate services. When all public libraries are fully staffed with those that value young adults, not only does the library thrive, but the community, of which adolescents are a part, thrives as well."[7]

If providing opportunity to learn is a main focus of the library mission, an opportunity to expand library staff's own knowledge horizons must be an integral component of that mission. A shift toward staff development and learning—moving from traditional ideas of training to more emerging approaches—will propel library staff into becoming the service providers that teens require. Frontline staff should be empowered to be at the forefront of this mission by advocating for more training opportunities and by communicating with local colleagues.

# Self-Assessment

Before starting or planning any professional development regimen, a self-assessment is one of the best ways to gain insight into personal learning needs. A look at learning goals and personal outlooks on learning can be illuminating. Within institutions, training can be made equitable by enabling self-assessment that addresses learning styles, skill level, core competencies, and motivation. Preparing staff for unexpected service encounters begins by having a strong understanding of each staff's individual motivations and learning styles.

The David P. Weikart Center for Youth Program Quality (CYPQ) offers a series of assessments for those working with youth.[8] These assessments focus on areas related to the environment in which youth learn, the interaction between youth and adults, resources available for learning, and so on. They also help those working with young people to reflect on what does and doesn't work in their youth-focused initiatives and make changes based on that assessment. CYPQ also trains practitioners working specifically with youth on how to use the assessments.[9] Through this training, youth-serving staff better understand where they need to learn more in order to better implement the assessments. In 2013 Ypsilanti Community Schools implemented the CYPQ's "Train the Trainer" curriculum. Social studies teacher Lauren Spoerl explained that the CYPQ "allowed me to reflect upon myself as an educator, improved student engagement, and has given me the resource to diversify classroom strategies to increase student retention of the content."[10] The assessment-based training opened a way for Spoerl to rethink her teaching style and provided opportunities for reflection, planning, and deeper teaching and learning engagement.

If a formal assessment is not yet feasible at your library, consider making time during a peer team or supervisory meeting to discuss ways of approaching continuous learning opportunities. Quality assessment pre- and post-tests can also serve as a way to report conference and professional training takeaways, either for personal use or practical application. Understanding your own learning needs can be a formidable undertaking. Everyone has inherent biases and blind spots, so it is important to not make any assumptions, including about ideas of your own training gaps.

Start from where you are right now, and think about your learning needs. The following questions can help guide a qualitative assessment of individual learning goals to prepare for training. Ask yourself:

- What are my individual strengths or talents that I bring to the profession?

- What are the barriers or challenges that I face in my profession?

- What is my learning style or approach to learning?

- What is my learning philosophy?

- How can I use that philosophy to approach professional training and development?

- What skills or competencies do I need in order to perform my job?

**Figure 1-1. Learning Organization Checklist**
Strategies for Everyone

1. Tolerate questions.

2. Think of knowledge as a strategy.

3. Learn to deal or negotiate with ideas.

4. Enjoy surprises.

5. Redefine your work as a resource for learning.

6. Be responsible.

7. Teach someone else.

*Source: How to Manage Training*

- What do I need from my organization to improve my job performance?

These questions and their answers can also be a method for opening a dialogue with frontline supervisors or managers who may not be aware of training gaps or opportunities.

Carolyn Nilson created a valuable reference guide to professional development in *How to Manage Training*.[11] This resource helps organizations strategize a potential overhaul of current training and offers an assessment for those who have successful training programs already in place. Nilson offers dozens of checklists that could be adapted to establish strategic, measurable, achievable, relevant, and time-oriented (SMART) goals for training initiatives. In the third edition of *How to Manage Training*, Nilson's "Learning Organization Checklist Strategies for Everyone" is a great launching point for any self-directed learner to consider before engaging in a continuous learning plan.

Nilson expands on this checklist as a way of cultivating questions, learning with compassion, seeing your work with fresh eyes, and viewing each work-related task as a learning opportunity. These are equally fantastic strategies for planning services for and with teens. Teens should feel that their individual learning goals are achievable through strong relationships with library staff. By the same measure, library staff at all

## Figure 1-2. IMLS 21st-Century Skills Assessment Framework

| Early Stage | Transitional Stage | 21st-Century Stage |
|---|---|---|
| Staff attends training opportunities as they are offered. | Staff demonstrates curiosity in a specific subject that relates to their job title. | Staff is engaged in a participatory training plan that is continuously adapting. |

*Source:* https://www.imls.gov/assets/1/AssetManager/21stCenturySkills.pdf.

levels should be given opportunities to gain trust and comfort working for and with teens.

The Institute of Museum and Library Services (IMLS) released a comprehensive self-assessment for organizations hoping to boost their staff teams with 21st-century skills development.[12] Though the assessment is focused on teams, the information could be easily adapted to fit the needs of an individual learner. The IMLS created a scalable process that begins at an early stage when staff are still developing, then moves to a transitional stage where the bulk of training takes place, and ends with a 21st-century stage that highlights the need for ongoing learning. Assessing your personal training needs in the context of 21st-century professional skills may help clarify specific training needs.

Sharing information from self-assessments and trainings should take place well beyond the walls of program evaluation, through quarterly or monthly check-in meetings, and beyond peer-group meetings or yearly reviews. In *Critical Knowledge Transfer*, researchers Dorothy Leonard-Barton, Walter Swap, and Gavin Barton from the *Harvard Business Review* detail strategy for knowledge-sharing collaborative programs known as "Knowledge Jams."[13] Colleagues gather and are given various scenarios, and the group problem-solves together. Another way of structuring a "Knowledge Jam" program is to invite participants to share anecdotal stories highlighting when they learned a new skill through an informal interaction.

> ## Figure 1-3. Professional Development Planning Checklist
>
> - Do you have random training opportunities or a specific plan for learning?
>
> - Have you articulated the differences between the concepts of orientation, training, development, and education?
>
> - Do you have an annual plan for learning or have you looked ahead two or three years to anticipate employee and organizational needs?
>
> - Does your organization typically train staff at random locations or have you designated learning workstations and specific environments for learning?
>
> - Do you schedule learning activities for a variety of times throughout the work week and month, or do you have self-directed, standardized, and scheduled learning times?
>
> - Do individual staff have specific learning plans?
>
> *Source:* Chapter 13 by Julie Todaro in *Staff Development: A Practical Guide,* Fourth Edition

# Developing a Future-Ready Continuous Learning Plan

To empower learning experiences that celebrate all levels of staffing and leadership, it is important to begin by creating a continuous learning agenda. Creating a learning agenda is similar to traditional training and professional development plans. Julie Todaro offers a checklist in "Planning a Training and Development Infrastructure for Library and Information Environments"[14] for improving the processes and quality of professional development for library staff:

Todaro's questions can spark a dialogue about continuous learning in the context of library staff training. While the answers may vary depending on budgetary constraints, the results are clear: Libraries must have intentional and specific strategic learning plans for all staff.

Lucretia Robertson, a training specialist in Washington State and a member of the Washington Library Trainers (WALT), explained in a recent interview that staff who are focused on professional development should bring information back to their teams and find ways to apply it to further learning.[15]

> Learning and training differ. Training is about building skills, and learning is about curiosity. Not everything is a training problem, so brainstorming ideas across staff levels is important. What I think needs to happen [is] a shift toward learning. [Libraries] are learning organizations—by default, but in some ways by design as well. For the most part, library staff are interested in learning and sharing. My hope is that we become a culture of learning, and by that I mean that we not only support a workforce that is constantly learning, but we are really in tune with how we can apply training, conference attendance, committee meetings, and our own personal interests, and apply them to practice.

As Robertson explained in our interview, staff are motivated by curiosity. This may mean learning outside of traditional training programs and/or by bringing in consultants to improve the overall employee engagement through the use of innovative training practices. Passionate library trainers can make an immense impact on empowering staff to get engaged in their own learning goals.

## 21st-Century Professional Skills

There are areas of need that staff might use as a foundation for their own learning. This foundation is built on skills that library staff already possess as providers of information and resources to a community; these skills are highlighted as a part of what the Partnership for 21st Century Learning (P21) identified as a comprehensive set of transferable skills that allow for college, career, and life readiness in the modern world. These are referred to as "21st Century Skills."[16] These skills can be categorized into three domains: cognitive, interpersonal, and intrapersonal.

- Cognitive skills build our knowledge and expertise; these skills help us understand our world and create meaningful connections to information.

- The highly collaborative teams of the 21st century call for interpersonal skills to communicate with our colleagues and to disseminate resources to library patrons.

- Intrapersonal skills are equally as important, giving us the ability to understand our processes and self-evaluate.

The 21st-century skills provide an essential focus for preparing staff to meet the demands of services for and with teens. The *Futures Report* calls for an expansion of these skills.

> [Library staff] must broaden their skills beyond programming and book talking to include training others, public speaking, collaboration, supervision, outcome measurement, facilitation, advocacy, and both project and change management skills. These professional skills, which are critical to the continued success of this work, must be taught in library and information science graduate schools and are necessary for continuing education for librarians already working.[17]

To successfully implement programs that prepare teens for their own skill development, staff must advance their own competencies in the workplace. The following sections look at professional skill areas and how they support the value of continuous learning by teen library staff.

## Knowledge

Library staff working with teens are knowledgeable about a wide array of topics. Their knowledge drives services that range from a traditional reference interview to facilitating a Spheros robot activity. As the needs of teens change and grow in the 21st century, library staff need to keep their knowledge up-to-date in order to facilitate the learning experiences that teens require. Library staff must honestly and continually analyze where their own knowledge gaps are when it comes to teen services and find ways to fill in those gaps. Asking questions like those listed below can help teen library staff better understand what they need to become knowledgeable about in order to serve the community successfully.

- What did I discover I needed to learn more about as a part of that last activity I took part in with teens?

- What do I need to know to improve my interactions with teens?

- What do I need to know in order to facilitate stronger learning experiences with and for teens?

## Creativity

The ability to be creative, imagine, and ideate multiple solutions to challenges is an extremely valuable skill in library services. Creativity is a key component to innovation, experimentation, and growth. Creative work adds to the authenticity of library services. As Ken Robinson explains in his 2001 book *Out of Our Minds*:

> Being creative is not a purely intellectual process. It may draw on all areas of human consciousness: on feelings, intuitions and being playfully imaginative, as well as on knowledge and practical skills. Creativity often taps into areas of consciousness that are not regulated by conscious thought. Our best ideas sometimes come to mind without our thinking consciously about them at all.[18]

Creativity can be a motivating factor in learning for library staff. Creativity lends itself to trial and error and "playing" around with different techniques and ideas. This idea of play as learning can be a challenge in the application of creativity to library work as play is often considered the antithesis of being professional and getting work done. Yet it's through play and creativity that true understanding may be achieved. In teen services, an example of integrating play and creativity in learning looks like this:

> Spending time with teens learning a new skill or technology. For example, if you have a new technology tool that teens are going to use, wait for the teens to start learning how to use that tool. Give the teens a chance to figure things out through trial and error and take part in that experience. You'll learn the technology as well as learn about how teens interact with new ideas and tools. This will give you a deeper understanding of teens and a better sense of the supports they need from the library.

## Collaboration

Collaboration is the art of doing, not by individual effort alone, but through a collective drive to work together. When it comes to continuous learning, collaboration is a powerful tool. An example of how collaboration and learning go together in teen library services is seen in YALSA's Future Ready with the Library (FRwtL) project. FRwtL is an IMLS-funded project that provides a yearlong learning experience to selected library staff in small, rural, and tribal libraries. The focus is on supporting the college- and career-readiness needs of middle school youth and their families. A web-based community of practice is a key part of the learning experience for participants, and within that community, small groups work together on various activities. As one participant wrote in the winter of 2016, "Had we worked on our own, each of us would have missed puzzle pieces."[19]

There are often challenges to successful learning-based collaboration. Sometimes everyone involved doesn't participate as is expected. The time it takes to collaborate might be more than what those in the group have to available. And those working to collaborate on learning might find that their goals do not align. For that reason, when collaborating on learning experiences, it's good to set ground rules and include time to talk with one another about expectations and goals. Don't forget to also talk about the tools you may use for collaborating—physical or technology based—to find out if everyone is comfortable with those and to determine if any further training in that area is required. Make sure to recognize the diverse skills that each member of the group brings to the collaborative learning experience. One way to do that is to have each person in the group talk about the one thing they think they could help others learn, and the one thing that each person would like to learn from someone else. This helps collaborators learn about each other's skills and also helps to create trust and respect for those working together on the learning experience.

## Adaptability

Adaptability enables 21st-century professionals to embrace failure and learn from mistakes. Learning is a continuous and sometimes messy endeavor, but library staff working with teens should not fear potential failure. One way of learning to be adaptable is to document a project over time. Note when you are having difficulties and write down your observations, questions, and, most importantly, when you get stuck. Revisit these notes and try to see if you find patterns. Asking yourself what helps you get unstuck or deal with stress is one way to improve your adaptability and a way to learn how to do an even better job next time.

## Leadership

Leadership takes place in a variety of settings and a variety of ways. For example, library staff working with teens might want to learn to be a leader within their organization in order to better champion teen services internally. Or, a teen-serving staff member might think it's time to learn how to be a leader in the local community taking part in different community projects and groups and helping to demonstrate the value of library teen services.

In 2016 the Coalition to Advance Learning in Archives, Libraries and Museums released the "Layers of Leadership Across Libraries, Archives and Museums." This document provides a framework for any teen library staff member who is planning for learning related to leadership. The document outlines six layers of leadership that one might work toward:

- Leading Self: focuses on expanding personal professional leadership opportunities

- Leading Others: focuses on working as a leader within a team setting

- Leading the Department: focuses on what it takes to demonstrate leadership within a management context

- Leading Multiple Departments: focuses on broadening leadership skills within an organization to take on more tasks and managing more projects and people.

- Leading the Organization: focuses on working as a leader in organizational culture and strategic directions

- Leading the Profession: focuses on taking a lead in helping the profession grow, change, and evolve.[20]

All of these require learning leadership skills. Some of the skills can be scaffolded from one layer to another, and some will come with entirely new learning experiences that lead to leadership. The Coalition to Advance Learning in Archives, Museums and Libraries has developed a set of training resources for those interested in learning how to be a more successful leader. These resources are available on the Coalition's website at http://www.coalitiontoadvancelearning.org/layers-leadership-framework-skills/.

# Engaging with Administrators on the Value of Continuous Learning

Teen staff in school and public libraries have the unique responsibility of advocating on behalf of youth; they also serve as the most immediate advocates for services that meet the needs of teens in local communities. In order to foster an environment that values the whole-library approach to services for and with teens, managers must also rise to the occasion or be brought into the conversation. Gaps in understanding the current needs of teens and techniques for successful library service to them are an underlying barrier that currently prevents forward movement in the field. Managers of frontline library staff can help to rectify this by supporting continuous learning and emphasizing the importance of adopting a growth mindset. In her book *Mindset*, Carol Dweck defines a growth mindset and a fixed mindset. As noted on the *Mindset* website:

> In a fixed mindset, people believe their basic qualities, like their intelligence or talent, are simply fixed traits. They spend their time documenting their intelligence or talent instead of developing them. They also believe that talent alone creates success—without effort. They're wrong. In a growth mindset, people believe that their most basic abilities can be developed through dedication and hard work—brains and talent are just the starting point. This view creates a love of learning and a resilience that is essential for great accomplishment. Virtually all great people have had these qualities.[21]

Applying some of Dweck's wisdom of growth mindsets versus fixed mindsets helps staff at all levels to understand the need to be continuously learning.

As much as the *Futures Report* is calling for a more connected approach to meeting community needs by listening to feedback from teens, it is also advocating for administrators to understand their role in supporting continuous learning. To meet the demands of providing excellent service for and with teens, a new management style may emerge that can lead the change: a connected manager. These powerful allies work alongside teen and school library staff who can leverage their power to make change happen, meeting with community partners, maintaining relationships with key stakeholders, and highlighting national guidelines for local impact. The connected manager is one who values continuous learning, embodies the 21st-century professional skills, is aware or even involved in professional learning networks, and continually assesses the culture of learning at a local level.

Possibly the most important quality of a connected manager is providing thoughtful feedback and assessment for frontline practitioners from a whole-library perspective. Rosalie Torres's *Evaluation Mindset for Continuous Learning* is based on the idea of the growth mindset and offers an approach for managers to use in evaluating staff learning.[22]

The "4 Processes of Continuous Learning" from Torres's diagram promotes an iterative and recurrent evaluation by way of asking questions, facilitating dialogue, examining underlying values, and reflecting on what you have learned. By applying this method to staff meetings, managers can increase the connectedness of their training and development plans for staff teams. Many libraries use evaluation and assessment to drive improvement of programs, products, and services.

Adrienne Breznau made positive changes in the connectedness of her team as the Public Services supervisor at the Sylvan Way branch of the Kitsap Regional Library in Washington. While she does not directly work with teens in her daily management of operations, she does see the impact that a connected community has on improving the overall conditions for teens. Adrienne has taken on a mindset of creating a connected workforce by opening training opportunities for staff that have traditionally not been involved in reference services, readers' advisory, or programming. She also emphasizes the whole-library approach by bringing together staff at all levels through monthly stand-up meetings that she calls "staff rallies." Her staff come together frequently to boost communication and break down barriers to collaboration. She said the idea came to her one day after receiving e-mails that all detailed a similar incident of communication breakdown. She wanted to act quickly and assertively to address the issue. "My reaction was to call an immediate mandatory meeting—but I took a step back and thought about how this action could be perceived and tried to think of a way to present a positive way to bring the staff back together. So I thought, 'What is a positive meeting like? How can I help the team rally around the idea of teamwork? A staff rally!'"[23] Breznau's eureka moment was set in motion, and the first of many innovative staff rallies was implemented. In addition to these monthly meetings, the daily communication and collaboration has broadened because of her connected learning practices.

Breznau's staff rallies are participatory and feature an open dialogue that improves engagement and communication. The structure is based on the idea of a monthly staff-manager meeting but in a group setting. It is separate from the one-on-one meetings Breznau holds monthly with each one of her staff. Everyone is expected to be present at the meeting, and there is a concise agenda that addresses quick wins and common goals. Breznau has worked with branch manager Leigh Ann Winterowd to incorporate a whole-library approach to the staff rallies by bringing in the public services team alongside many special branches including adult services, youth services, and even human resources staff. The impact is a the boost in communication and collaboration, while lending creativity to problem solving and learning from one another.

This may seem like an enormous undertaking for frontline staff and for library resources, but implementing more communication has many added benefits. Taking all of the staff from their frontline positions for a two-hour meeting can be a nearly impossible endeavor, both for staff to be away from their work and for those covering the service points. Breznau prepares for the staff rally by recruiting coverage for all frontline service points so that all staff are able to attend. While it may not be applicable to all library settings, there may be elements of the staff rally approach that could be transferred to other libraries in need of more communication, which can lead to learning between staff and management.

## Innovation as Learning

In 2015, Amy K. Garmer published a comprehensive guide to the Aspen Institute Leadership Roundtable discussions centered on library innovation. The ideas from this meeting have spearheaded a discussion of the library's role in creating cultures of innovation. Garmer's report, "Libraries in the Exponential Age: Moving from the Edge of Innovation to the Center of Community," argues that innovation in the library is traditionally on the edge of the organization rather than the core.[24]

> Innovation provides a competitive advantage in a knowledge-based economy. Libraries have the potential to be platforms for innovation and entrepreneurial activity in the community. However, like the community itself, libraries must foster a culture of innovation and look to ways to foster new thinking and experimentation at the edges of institutions and connect them to the centers.[25]

Furthermore, the case studies that leaders discussed at the Leadership Roundtable on Library Innovation demonstrate that libraries have the opportunity to be on the forefront of advancement. Bringing innovation back to the center of the library can unlock potential for community engagement. Garmer's report raises a very important question in relation to balancing divergent thought and staff capacity: Frontline library staff are busy, so how can we make time to innovate?

The idea of innovation on work time is not a new phenomenon. When the U.S. stock market crashed in 1929, a surprising problem-solving innovation emerged at engineering company 3M that allowed employees to use a percentage of their work time to devote to special projects. This forward-thinking practice became known as "15% Time" and led to some of 3M's most successful products. Les Krogh started working at 3M in 1948, when 15% time was fully implemented into work schedules. During his years as vice president, he stated that innovation time was typically met with cynicism. "They couldn't understand how we could allow people 15% of their time to do what they wanted and still meet important deadlines. It was inconceivable that we would permit so much freedom." Yet the practice remains a central part of 3M's philosophy, even today. It inspired great ideas, like 3M Post-It Notes and Scotch tape, which have been able to stick around.[26]

Similar models of innovation were created at the Center for Creative Leadership, where Morgan McCall and colleagues came up with the "70:20:10 Model for Learning and Development."[27] In this equation, 70% of focused work time is devoted to tasks where staff can work in conditions that are optimal for flow—a phenomenon that is experienced when work is both engaging and challenging. Then 20% of work time is used for feedback and meetings. And finally 10% is used for formal learning. In 2005 Google's Eric Schmidt adapted the ratio into a resource management model.[28] Schmidt's model drove system-level approach to innovation at Google. Some of Google's greatest products, like Gmail and Google Maps, are a result of 20% time,[29] which allows engineers to pursue personally rewarding independent projects.

Libraries are adopting the 20% time formula to create continuous learning environments for staff. In 2013 WebJunction, an online source of professional development webinars for library staff, featured innovative speakers from the Tooele City Library in Utah. This library created a foundational Self-Directed Achievement Model, which is based on the concept of expecting staff to set one training goal a week that is achievable in one hour. This learning happy hour has created a mechanism that is a "consistent, agile, individualized approach to staff development in a climate of constant change. It champions the basic library principle of lifelong learning. It is achievable for every individual with any level of expertise."[30] Jami Carter, director of Tooele City Library, highlighted the achievement of her staff who use their learning hour to increase competencies in e-book devices, research guides, and databases, resulting in increased confidence.[31]

# Tools for Learning

## Micro-Credentials and Digital Badges

Earning credentials in a field outside of your daily work parameters can be a challenge if you do not have time for formal learning experiences. Informal learning settings may not be able to issue transferable credits, but may be able to demonstrate tangible evidence of an individual's skills. Built on the connected learning framework,[32] badging systems enable non-experts to gain and demonstrate skill sets. Digital badges are a kind of micro-credential that can be earned through self-directed continuous learning.

In 2012 the MacArthur Foundation and the Mozilla Foundation partnered to create the Open Badges system.[33] The infrastructure for badges is open source and freely available. Unlike accreditation systems in formal learning settings that have a limit on gaining knowledge, Open Badges can be continually earned with no exceptions. Erin Knight, a Badge Alliance liaison, documented this key difference in a working paper during the project to create Open Badges.

> [Badges] can play a crucial role in the connected learning ecology by acting as a bridge between contexts and making these alternative learning channels, skills and types of learning more viable, portable and impactful. Badges can be awarded for a potentially limitless set of individual skills regardless of where each skill is developed, and the collection of badges can serve as a virtual resume of competencies and qualities for key stakeholders such as peers, schools or potential employers.[34]

Henry Jenkins introduced participatory micro-credentials in 2006.[35] Jenkins suggests that badges are connected to an emerging informal curriculum that values "forms of participatory culture, including opportunities for peer-to-peer learning, a changed attitude toward intellectual property, the diversification of cultural expression, the development of skills valued in the modern workplace, and a more empowered conception of citizenship." Jenkins explains that informal learning settings provided the greatest potential for tapping into participatory learning.

Digital badging systems have enormous potential for application in continuous learning practices. In professional practice, as Mark Aberdour examined, badges can be used as educational architecture for workplace learning.[36] While many digital badging systems are currently being used in public services, a case can be made for the added value of including badges for professional development.

The Badge Alliance Professional Development work group was created to address Open Badges in a training and development context. In 2015 the group began working toward employer acceptance of badges.[37] The work of sustaining Open Badges is ongoing, yet the infrastructure that is in place could potentially serve as evidence-based professional development for informal learning on the job.

## Learning Playlists

Learning playlists are thematic narratives for learning that guide someone through a given subject. Some libraries use similar formats—LibGuides, for example—to provide context to any given subject. Playlists are very similar. A learning playlist is essentially a group of bookmarks—from videos, articles, webinars, tags, and other media outlets—that are remixed to create a lesson plan for learners.

LNRG explains the benefit of learning playlists in their "Partner Handbook[38]: "The power of playlists lies in the opportunity for collaboration. Although one organization can design a sequence based on internal goals, multiple providers can work together to include many types and sources of learning. These collaborative playlists create a rich network of experiences for learners."[39]

Playlists can be used as an entry point into a new subject or as a way to revisit information. Additionally, library administrators can use learning playlists to share knowledge that informs an organization's strategic goal.

## Cultures of Learning

Continuous learning requires a great deal of perseverance, particularly when the learning taking place is self-directed. Keeping up your personal momentum can be a real challenge for any learning endeavor. To combat work-related fatigue and information overload, there are several strategies that staff can use to continue their learning goals that can be applied to online networks. It is essential to understand that online systems are unpredictable and will change, expand, become irrelevant, or cease to exist. Try cultivating your 21st-century professional skills by engaging in national discussions on social networks or sharing your training with local colleagues and administrators.

## Connected Learning Networks

Connected learning is a framework that drives professional dialogue surrounding continuous learning programs and gives avenues for professionals to share ideas, feedback, and iterative design. By connecting the personal and professional learning that staff are engaging in, more dialogue can happen at the local level. For example, after attending an inspiring conference, try hosting a training session, for your colleagues, based on the major takeaways from the conference. Bring in examples that are relevant to your local community. Scaling for local impact is what communities of practice are best used for in application, both on the local stage and globally through online networks. Professional organizations also help to bring together regional networks of libraries, museums, school districts, nonprofits, small businesses, and government.

Connecting formal and informal learning experiences can be the catalyst for communities to engage in local connected learning networks. In 2013 Cathy Lewis Long and Matt Hannigan of the Sprout Fund established the Pittsburgh (PA) Hive Learning Network.[40] The Hive launched ten local projects in Pittsburgh, and connected school districts with out-of-school-time learning experiences.[41] These projects led to a local network of out-of-school program providers known as the Remake Learning Network, a professional network that brings together educators and innovators in the Pittsburgh region.[42] A movement began to grow as more practitioners and members of the public became connected through community learning programs. The connected learning network in this city provided "global connections with hyper local experiences."[43] Lewis Long and Hannigan began to notice a trend of obstacles facing youth workers in the Pittsburgh Hive Learning Network. "The practitioners in these settings don't have the professional development to teach digital literacy skills and they don't have the necessary tools and resources."[44] Despite being geographically focused on the greater Pittsburgh region, the amount of resources, organizations, and training tools could be useful on a national scale. For practitioners in Pittsburgh, being introduced to this network and the potential for learning could seem daunting. To close the training gap, Lewis Long and Hannigan developed the Remake Learning Network's Digital Corps team, focused on training youth workers with the connected learning network in Pittsburgh to train and deploy new literacies. "We saw it as a great way to advance learning and scaffold it in ways that are fun, while at the same time not expecting more from the educators who are working in those informal spaces than they are actually able to deliver."[45]

The Digital Corps is a group of professionals who gain strong levels of competencies in emerging technologies and assist out-of-school-time programs to advance their learning outcomes. The Digital Corps become proficient in digital media learning technologies and open source software. As peer leaders in the Remake Learning Network, these professionals take their training to out-of-school program practitioners.[46]

In 2014 members of the Digital Corps worked together to co-create a digital badging platform for the entire city. With the engagement of more than 100 educators from the region, seven major competencies for programs emerged that were aligned with 21st-century skills development.[47]

Communities of practice are strengthened by founding strong local networks of professional organizations that share common values and goals. Scaffolding local partnerships with learning opportunities reveals the promising prospect of fostering cultures of learning. Maintaining the motivation of continuous learners begins by encouraging staff to engage in creating an organizational culture of learning where ideas are shared, remixed, and applied in practice.

# Taking Your Learning to the World through Personal Branding

Whether you are fresh on the library scene or demonstrating years of experience, documenting your service and training is a transferable skill that can greatly benefit your continuous learning plan. It is not about selling yourself by selling out; or as Marc Ecko elegantly puts it, "A brand is made of blood and bones, skin, and organs. A brand has a heartbeat."[48] Personal branding is a reflection of yourself—your ideals, your values, and your ethics regarding the kind of work that you do; a personal brand is deeply rooted in your authentic experience. Every cover letter or teaching philosophy, curriculum vitae, or résumé that you create is an expression of your personal brand. Demonstrating in your branding that you are a continuous learner enables you to connect with other educators in the field. It is one step toward entering a connected learning network.

There are many ways you can develop your sense of self. Whether you are using a personality test, creative expression, digital portfolios, or even business cards, finding ways to connect with others starts with a strong understanding of why you want to make an impact in the first place. Think about how you can provide services in a unique way, or how you might iterate on an evolving solution in your community; think about how you want to share your ideas nationally and locally with like-minded organizations. Simon Sinek's *Start with Why* provides a series of questions to help you get started in this:

- What are my personal and professional goals?

- What services are available in my community? What are not available?

- What services can I provide with the capacity that I have?

- What project would I want to do for my community if I had all the means?

- How will I be able to meet the needs of my community?

- Why am I interested in services for and with teens in my community?

- In what unique way can I advocate for the services the library provides?[49]

Try to connect these questions back to your local community, and let your answers help you understand what you still need to learn. Although branding is largely something that has evolved on the public stage, it can also help you define your role in the local knowledge economy. Think about the networks of educators, nonprofit organizations, or businesses that have goals aligned to your own—as library staff, if you understand your goals, you can connect the dots between these missions.

Bohyun Kim noticed a trend within the New Member Round Table (NMRT) of the American Library Association. Ideas were converging in discussions surrounding the use of social media platforms for professional development. What emerged was a dialogue on library staff professional identities and personal branding.

Andromeda Yelton, a technologist at Unglue.It, was one of the featured speakers at the NMRT's Personal Branding panel. When Yelton started her job search in a very competitive market, she decided that she needed a way to make herself stand out from the multitudes of candidates. Yelton created a personal inventory of her unique skills and used this list to fine-tune how she presented herself to potential employers.[50] Yelton focused on evidence-based branding, a method she describes as using digital platforms to demonstrate credentials and provide contextual examples of her technical skills.

After the NMRT discussion, Kim explained to *American Libraries* magazine that "personal branding is about acknowledging the fact that information about us online will inevitably represent us to others whether we like it or not and involves consciously taking charge of that information ourselves."[51] There are vast arrays of library blogs, podcasts, and social media collectives that are shaping the profession. Personal branding can be a way of demonstrating employability and connecting with geographically distant colleagues, as well as a helpful tool for professional development.

Buffy Hamilton, a library blogger known as "the Unquiet Librarian," was able to make a significant career transition that was aided in part by her personal branding. She documented her experience over seven years as a school librarian and used her blog platform to discuss education in the library field.[52] By sharing her knowledge, trials, and errors, Hamilton was able to reach broad audiences and contribute to staff learning in both public and school libraries. Hamilton earned recognition for her contributions to the library profession as a *Library*

*Journal* "Mover and Shaker." Eventually, her blog transcended the personal sphere of her own work and became a forum for school library staff to speak up in comments to posts that were relevant to their training needs.

In many ways, *The Unquiet Librarian* blog is as much a personal brand as it is a training tool for library staff in schools and public libraries. Hamilton continues to share her personal knowledge and passion through her blog. By continuing to maintain this resource over several years and sharing her insights, Hamilton is able to continually teach and learn with her professional learning network.

Individuals who are designing their own professional identity by personal branding exemplify the benefits of continuous learning. Learning networks are strengthened by individuals who understand their inherent biases, privileges, knowledge base, training gaps, and learning needs. By having a grasp of who you are as a learner and how you relate to your learning network, your brand will transcend from merely a self-promotional device to a powerful networking tool.

# Keep Learning

Continuous learning is essential to successfully implementing teen library services. Continuous learning is not pinned to a specific kind of technology, but is constantly evolving with advancements of the field. To reach the full extent of the envisioned future, libraries in the present should invest in the continuous learning efforts of staff. Libraries foster unique lifelong learning environments, and the same advantages should be afforded to library staff at all levels. Learning is the key to unlocking the potential of a dynamic and connected library workforce.

Continuous learning requires a mindset that enables library staff to constantly expand their skills and approaches. In the envisioned future of the YALSA *Futures Report*, library administration will emphasize the importance of continuous learning as a benefit to employees and to the overall health of library organizations. Library staff who are working with teens lead the whole-library approach to improving services and serve as coaches for their colleagues. Staff understand their unique roles in creating learning environments within their community by continuing to develop their own skills. The Futures Report demystified the role of staff in the future information landscape. It is not a choice between innovation and irrelevance. Library-driven change will drive the future so long as we never stop learning.

# Notes

1. U.S. Census Bureau, "Estimates of US and Territories Populations" (raw data), July 1, 2015, Factfinder.census.gov/bkmk/table/1.0/en/PEP/2015/PEPAGE-SEX?slice= GEO~0100000US (accessed February 21, 2017).

2. Bill Scher, "Bush vs. Obama on the Economy in 3 Simple Charts: Updated," OurFuture.org, December 8, 2014, https://ourfuture.org/20141208/bush-vs-obama-on-the-economy-in-3-simple-charts (accessed February 21, 2017).

3. Graham R. Cochran and Theresa M. Ferrari, "Preparing Youth for the 21st Century Knowledge Economy: Youth Programs and Workforce Preparation," *Afterschool Matters* 8 (Spring 2009): 11–25, http://www.robertbownefounda-tion.org/pdf_files/2009_asm_spring.pdf (accessed February 21, 2017).

4. Annie E. Casey Foundation, *Kids Count Data Book: State Trends in Child Well-Being 2016*, 2016, http://www.aecf.org/m/resourcedoc/aecf-the2016k-idscountdatabook-2016.pdf (accessed February 21, 2017).

5. John B. Horrigan, *Digital Readiness Gaps*, Pew Research Center, September 20, 2016, http://www.pewinternet.org/2016/09/20/digital-readiness-gaps/ (accessed February 21, 2017).

6. Linda W. Braun, Maureen L. Hartman, Sandra Hughes-Hassell, and Kafi Ku-masi, *The Future of Library Services for and with Teens: A Call to Action* (IMLS and YALSA, January 2014), http://www.ala.org/yaforum/sites/ala.org.yaforum/files/content/YALSA_nationalforum_final.pdf (accessed February 21, 2017).

7. Linda W. Braun, "The Importance of a Whole Library Approach to Public Library Young Adult Services: A YALSA Issue Paper," January 8, 2011, http://www.ala.org/yalsa/guidelines/whitepapers/wholelibrary (accessed February 21, 2017).

8. David P. Weikart Center for Youth Program Quality, "Youth Program Quality Assessment® and School-Age Program Quality Assessment," http://www.cypq.org/assessment (accessed February 21, 2017).

9. David P. Weikart Center for Youth Program Quality, "Approach," http://cypq.org/about/approach (accessed February 21, 2017).

10. David P. Weikart Center for Youth Program Quality, "Methods Training Helps Teachers in the Classroom," *Program Quality News*, November 2013, http://cypq.org/sites/cypq.org/files/PDFs%20of%20Monthly%20Newsletter/Pro-

gram%20Quality%20News%20October%202013.pdf (accessed February 22, 2017).

11. Carolyn Nilson, *How to Manage Training: A Guide to Design and Delivery for High Performance* (AMACOM/American Management Association, 2007).

12. Institute of Museum and Library Services, "Self-Assessment Tool for Museums, Libraries, and 21st Century Skills," 2015, https://www.imls.gov/sites/default/files/publications/thumbs/21stcenturyskills_matrix_print.pdf (accessed February 22, 2017).

13. Dorothy Leonard-Barton, Walter C. Swap, and Gavin B. Barton, *Critical Knowledge Transfer: Tools for Managing Your Company's Deep Smarts* (Boston: Harvard Business Review Press, 2015).

14. Julie Todaro, "Planning a Training and Development Infrastructure for Library and Information Environments: Roles and Responsibilities," in *Staff Development: A Practical Guide*, 4th ed., ed. Andrea Wigbels Stewart, Carlette Washington-Hoagland, and Carol T. Zsulya (Chicago: American Library Association, 2013).

15. Lucretia Robertson, in discussion with the author, June 2016.

16. Bernie Trilling and Charles Fadel, *21st Century Skills: Learning for Life in Our Times* (New York: John Wiley & Sons, 2012).

17. Braun et al., *The Future of Library Services*, p. 24.

18. Ken Robinson, *Out of Our Minds: Learning to Be Creative* (Oxford: Capstone Publishing, 2001), p. 78.

19. Participant comment, hq.yalsa.net (closed community of practice), February 10, 2017.

20. David Horth, Anne Ackerson, Carol Jenkins, Cal Shepherd, Rita Van Duinen, Susan Perry, Christie Hill, and Christine Drummond, "Nexus LAB: Layers of Leadership Across Libraries, Archives and Museums—September 2016 Draft," https://educopia.org/sites/educopia.org/files/deliverables/NexusLab_LayersOfLeadership_DraftFinal091416c.pdf (accessed February 21, 2017).

21. Carol S. Dweck, "What Is Mindset," *Mindset*, https://mindsetonline.com/whatisit/about/index.html (accessed February 22, 2017).

22. Kelly Hannum, Jennifer Martineau, and Claire Reinelt, eds., *The Handbook of Leadership Development Evaluation* (San Francisco: Jossey-Bass, 2007).

23. Adrienne Breznau, in discussion with the author, July 2016.

24. Amy K. Garmer, *Libraries in the Exponential Age: Moving from the Edge of Innovation to the Center of Community* (Aspen Institute, 2016), https://cs-reports.aspeninstitute.org/documents/Libraries_Exponential_Age.pdf (accessed February 22, 2017).

25. Ibid., p. 10.

26. 3M, *A Century of Innovation: The 3M Story* (3M Company, 2002), http://multimedia.3m.com/mws/media/171240O/3m-coi-book-tif.pdf (accessed February 22, 2017).

27. Michael M. Lombardo and Robert W. Eichinger, *The Career Architect Development Planner: A Systematic Approach to Development Including 103 Research-Based and Experience-Tested Development Plans and Coaching Tips; for Learners, Managers, Mentors, and Feedback Givers* (Minneapolis: Lominger International, 2010).

28. Eric Schmidt and Jonathan Rosenberg, *Google: How Google Works* (London: John Murray, 2015).

29. Alex K., "Google's 20% Time in Action," Google *Official Blog*, May 18, 2006, https://googleblog.blogspot.com/2006/05/googles-20-percent-time-in-action.html (accessed February 22, 2017).

30. Betha Gutsche, "Self-Directed Achievement on a Small Scale," *WebJunction*, April 5, 2016, http://www.webjunction.org/news/webjunction/self-directed-achievement.html (accessed February 22, 2017).

31. Susan Green, "A Happy Hour for Library Staff Learning," *WebJunction*, July 30, 2013, http://www.webjunction.org/news/webjunction/happy-hour-for-library-staff-learning.html (accessed February 22, 2017).

32. "Why Connected Learning," *Educator Innovator*, http://educatorinnovator.org/why-connected-learning/ (accessed February 22, 2017).

33. "Discover Open Badges," *Open Badges*, http://openbadges.org/ (accessed February 22, 2017).

34. Peer 2 Peer University, the Mozilla Foundation, and the MacArthur Foundation, "An Open Badge System Framework," https://wiki.mozilla.org/images/f/f3/OpenBadges_--_Working_Badge_Paper.pdf (accessed February 22, 2017).

35. Henry Jenkins, *Confronting the Challenges of Participatory Culture: Media Education for the 21st Century* (Cambridge, MA: MIT Press, 2009).

36. Mark Aberdour, "Transforming Workplace Learning Culture with Digital Badges," in *Foundation of Digital Badges and Micro-Credentials*, ed. Dirk Ifenthaler, Nicole Bellin-Mularski, and Dana-Kristin Mah (Springer International Publishing, 2016), 203–19.

37. "Badges for Educators & Professional Development Badges," *Badge Alliance*, http://www.badgealliance.org/badges-educators-professional-development/ (accessed February 22, 2017).

38. LRNG, *Partner Handbook v.1.1: Your Guide to Creating XPs, Playlists, and Badges*, https://dmlcompetition.net/wp-content/themes/dml6/pdfs/LRNG_PartnerHandbook_v1.1.1.pdf (accessed February 22, 2017).

39. LRNG, https://www.lrng.org/ (accessed February 22, 2017).

40. "Sprout Receives Grant to Launch New Corps of Digital Learning Experts," *The Sprout Fund*, http://www.sproutfund.org/2013/08/13/sprout-receives-grant-to-launch-new-corps-of-digital-learning-experts/ (accessed February 22, 2017).

41. "Hive Learning Network Pittsburgh," *Hive Pittsburgh*, http://hivepgh.sprout-fund.org/ (accessed February 22, 2017).

42. "Resources," *Remake Learning*, October 16, 2014, http://remakelearning.org/collection/resources-2/ (accessed February 22, 2017).

43. "Supporting Learning Innovation at the Local Level: A Few Moments with Cathy Lewis Long and Matt Hannigan," *DML Hub*, http://dmlhub.net/newsroom/expert-interviews/supporting-learning-innovation-at-a-local-level/ (accessed February 22, 2017).

44. Ibid.

45. Ibid.

46. Ani Martinez, "Digital Corps: Activating Digital Literacies in Out-of-School Settings." *Remake Learning*, January 4, 2017, http://remakelearning.org/project/digital-corps/ (accessed February 22, 2017).

47. Remake Learning, *Playbook: Building Collaborative Interactive Networks for Teaching and Learning* (Pittsburgh: Sprout Fund, October 2015), http://downloads.sproutfund.org/playbook/remake-learning-playbook-20151022.pdf (accessed February 22, 2017).

48. Marc Ecko, *Unlabel: Selling You without Selling Out* (New York: Touchstone, 2015).

49. Simon Sinek, "Learn Your Why," *Start with Why*, https://www.startwithwhy.com/LearnYourWhy.aspx (accessed February 22, 2017).

50. Andromeda Yelton, "ALA11 Takeaways," *Andromeda Yelton: Across Divided Networks*, July 2, 2011, https://andromedayelton.com/2011/07/02/ala11-takeaways/ (accessed February 22, 2017).

51. Karen Schneider, "Personal Branding for Librarians: Distinguishing Yourself from the Professional Herd," *American Libraries*, November 6, 2012, https://americanlibrariesmagazine.org/2012/11/06/personal-branding-for-librarians/ (accessed February 22, 2017).

52. Buffy Hamilton, "About Me," *The Unquiet Librarian*, https://theunquietlibrarian.wordpress.com/about/ (accessed February 22, 2017).

LOUISVILLE FREE PUBLIC LIBRARY (KY)

# Kentucky Youth Film Festival

TRACY THOMAS

## What Did You Want to Achieve?

At the Louisville Free Public Library we want to give teens a venue to show their creativity to the broader Louisville community. By partnering with the Louisville International Festival of Films on the Kentucky Youth Film Festival, we provide teens of all filmmaking levels—from those shooting on phone cameras to those at magnet schools working with high-end video equipment—the chance to be a part of a city-wide event that celebrates their talents and skills

## Overview of the Program/Project

In the fall we co-sponsor, with the Louisville International Festival of Films, the Kentucky Youth Film Festival. High school students are encouraged to submit their films, which are judged by a group of librarians, teachers, and film industry professionals. Selected films are awarded prizes. Teens in 9th through 12th grade are invited to submit in one of three categories: Public Service Announcement, Documentary, or

Short Film. Also, writer/ producer Matt Berman adds a special category for youth entries. In 2015 Berman's theme was bullying. In 2016 Berman's category focused on teens creating a film inspired by an original piece of music (pre-selected by Berman). The awards ceremony is held at the Main Branch of the Louisville Free Public Library. The top three films in each category are shown and awards presented. Louisville-born actor Conrad Bachman (Louisville International Film Festival founder) is on hand to assist in the awards ceremony.

## What Challenges Did you Face and How Did You Overcome Them?

We struggle with making sure that teens who would be interested in this program know that it's available to them. In 2016 we collaborated with Beargrass Media and held a week-long film camp at the Main Library. Patrick Fitzgerald, the owner of Beargrass Media, planned and presented the week-long event. Almost 20 teens came to learn and experience filmmaking. Many professionals came to teach sessions about acting, cameras, public speaking, field audio, and post-production. The teens also took tours around Louisville, visiting a radio station, a news station, and the local newspaper.

In an effort to inform more library staff, as entries in the Festival don't have to be from Louisville teens, I presented on the program at the Kentucky Library Association Conference. My goal in this presentation was to get word out state-wide about the program so that more teens would learn what was available to them.

## What Did You Learn?

I am continually inspired by how teens rise to the Youth Film Festival challenge and demonstrate their great talents.

## How Does This Work Connect to YALSA's Futures Report and Vision?

The YALSA *Future of Library Services for and with Teens: A Call to Action* report speaks to the need for libraries to support connected learning by providing opportunities for teens to connect to their passions and interests through library activities. By giving teens in Louisville (and Kentucky) an entry into film world, we are doing just that.

We also connect to the Futures Report by collaborating with other city organizations. Our partnership with the Film Festival helps demonstrate that the Library is a city agency interested in supporting teen needs inside and outside of our library buildings.

## ZION-BENTON PUBLIC LIBRARY (IL)

# Connecting with Teens through Personal Interests

ELISE MARTINEZ

## What Did You Want to Achieve?

Bikes and skateboards are how the teens in the Zion-Benton Public Library community get around. Through hands-on demonstrations teens gained a deeper understanding about the mechanics of their bikes and skateboards and how they work. By exposing them to this information, we looked to empower teens with the tools to maintain their own transportation methods, putting them in control and reducing future maintenance costs. We also wanted teens to see us as a resource for all their needs, including athletics and transportation.

## Overview of the Program/Project

The Zion-Benton Public Library is situated in an economically disadvantaged community. Most of the teen population relies heavily on their bikes as their main method of transportation. In order to support teen needs and interests related to their mode of transportation, we hosted a series of programs about bike repair and maintenance.

For our first program we partnered with our local bike shop. In this program teens learned the basics of patching and changing a flat, fixing a popped chain, and bike maintenance tricks. We finished the program with a professional stunt team BMX demonstration. Teens really enjoyed seeing professional bikers perform. Following the performance the team welcomed participants conversation about their work and bikes.

For our second program we invited a local sports academy to lead a skateboard workshop. The instructors worked with teens to show them how to use a skateboard, perform basic tricks, and maintain their boards. This program was also an opportunity to highlight library nonfiction materials related to the program focus.

## What Challenges Did You Face and How Did You Overcome Them?

Effective outreach has historically been an issue for our library. We realized very early on that we needed to be present where our teens were, which is in the schools. By utilizing the support of teachers and school staff, we were able to spread the word about our workshops and resources better than if we tried to do it simply from within our building.

Another issue we face is pushing through the stereotype of a library as a quiet place where patrons only read books or use the computer. Our library has dramatically evolved over the past few years, and our community is still catching up. By continuing to offer programs that veer outside of meeting strictly reading-related needs, we have seen members of our community, namely teens, using our library to connect to their interests.

## What Did You Learn?

After our BMX stunt performance we noticed that many attendees went up to talk to the bikers. This opportunity to connect with an adult role model was important to the success of the program. We want to continue offering these opportunities for teens to connect to the outside world through positive adult mentorship.

# How Does This Work Connect to YALSA's Futures Report and Vision?

Partnering with local businesses connected teens to the wider community and allowed them to engage with other adult mentors and educators. Positive adult interactions provide teens with a vision and context for their future. Also, the Teen Services staff at the Zion-Benton Public Library use the connected learning model to structure and guide our programming, specifically when it comes to library staff serving as connectors between teens and learning. By hosting programs that support the engagement and growth of our teens, we empower them to take charge of their future; having the skills necessary to maintain their own bikes and skateboards ensures their independence. Through these programs, we hoped to make our teen population aware of the types of programs and services that we offer. Programs that not only meet the needs of our 21st century teens, but programs that provide the assistance and learning they need to be successful adults. Sometimes that can be as simple as learning how to fix your own bike or skateboard.

# CHAPTER 2
# Supporting Youth Learning

CRYSTLE MARTIN

## Introduction

Powerful learning for teens is learning that is integrated throughout a young person's life. Learning does not have to be isolated strictly within formal educational settings such as school classrooms. Learning outside of formal structures is as important as learning in formal environments. Informal settings can provide youth with a wider variety of opportunities to connect with topics and resources that support their personal passions and interests.

Library staff who serve teens have an opportunity to play an important role in youth learning in informal settings. Programming should help expand youth learning horizons and offer opportunities to build life skills such as problem solving, critical thinking, and collaboration. Teens can be motivated by their interests and passions just as much as, if not more than, by fun, and that's why library programs and activities should be based on teens' interests rather than simply focused on having fun. Ultimately, libraries offer an excellent option to tie together the informal learning that youth do in purely interest-driven spaces with the formal learning of school.

This chapter explores teen informal learning and how it can be supported by library staff. It begins with a discussion of informal and interest-driven learning, which is followed by a discussion of the barriers that exist for youth when it comes to informal and interest-driven learning. The focus then turns to how informal learning can be connected to teens' larger learning ecosystem. Finally, the chapter closes with a description of how library staff can and do support youth learning.

# Interest-Driven Learning

Interest-driven learning has been studied in both semi-formal and informal spaces. Researchers looking at informal learning environments discovered that learning in this way occurs both as general learning—for example, developing communication skills—and as discipline-specific learning, such as learning physics.[1] Interest-driven learning takes place anywhere youth can pursue one or more of their interests, and it offers young people the opportunity to develop expertise and agency, as well as disciplinary skills. For teens, interest-driven learning experiences offer the opportunity to be recognized as an expert, which is often unavailable in other settings in which teens spend time. It's possible to see the value of this type of learning by looking at video game and DIY communities.

## Video Game Communities

Existing research demonstrates that through participation in video game communities, youth develop math, science reasoning, emerging literacy, and reading skills. In part this is because of access to peer support and online resources. World of Warcraft (WoW), a massively multiplayer online game (MMO), is one example. In this game, players develop information skills as they navigate the *constellation of information* that is a part of the game, in order to solve a variety of complex problems. Reading research shows that youth who participate in this game play demonstrate with high accuracy at and above grade level when reading World of Warcraft materials.[2] This is particularly true for youth who are known to struggle to read at grade level. Youth use socially created WoW game resources to search for game-related information. It's clear that in game play of this type, youth-initiated information seeking supports youth aspirations for learning and skill development.[3]

Similarly, English-language learners (ELLs) demonstrate that through writing World of Warcraft fan fiction, they improve their English. This is because they are able to practice in a low-stakes, interest-driven situation with the support of peers who provide critical, constructive feedback.[4] Beyond reading and writing, Constance Steinkuehler and Caroline Williams found that WoW players blend narrative and math as a way to build "rhetorically persuasive models" to convince players of their solution to a problem.[5] This demonstrates how players develop critical thinking and logic skills and use them in everyday experiences.

Participation in video game communities can also be used as a place to try out and move forward with career paths. For example, Amanda Ochsner describes how fans of video games who write fan fiction and participate on wikis connect these skills to career paths.[6] For example, one teen used her fan fiction writing as a way to build confidence and skills as a writer while she was planning for her life after high school.

It's clear that many collaborative activities that support learning and lifelong decision making occur in video game communities: collective problem solving, adopting multiple roles, confronting ineffective strategies and misconceptions, and providing collaborative work skills; all are useful to participants beyond experiences in the community.[7] Video game communities provide a space where a group can get together and peer-to-peer and contextual learning takes place.

## DIY

Do-It-Yourself (DIY) communities also offer opportunities for interest-driven, informal learning. These communities have much in common with video game communities because they usually have a shared purpose and much effort is put into problem solving and skill development within them. DIY communities use the collective intelligence of the group to provide and access vast amounts of knowledge and expertise about specific aspects of their community. Knitting communities, like Ravelry,[8] are a great example of learning in an out-of-school DIY online community.

Ravelry is an online community for those interested in fiber crafting. Participants gather on Ravelry to share their products; to learn skills such as knitting, crocheting, and spinning; to learn how to create patterns and share their results; and to get help with problems they run into while crafting. Together the community has more knowledge and expertise than any one local group could have, and it makes that knowledge and expertise accessible to people no matter how physically isolated they are from other fiber crafters, fostering opportunities for learning that might not otherwise develop.

DIY encompasses communities and activities such as makerspaces and creative coding (creating a game, for example, with code). They act as a place where people of shared interests come together to find social support and help with skill development. A large DIY community is the Scratch community. Scratch supports social creating and learning of a variety of contexts including computational thinking and coding.[9] In the Scratch community, and in other DIY communities, participants develop flexibility and fluency, critical reflection through creative media production, and the digital equivalent of the functional literacies of reading and writing.

# Interest-Based Learning Challenges

Some challenges remain for teen informal interest-driven learning opportunities. Frequently, these are due to lack of access to these opportunities and to the technology required to participate, especially for those from low-income communities.

## Teen Media Access and Use

The discussion of gaming and DIY communities highlights the need to have access to technology to participate fully in interest-based informal learning. For many youth, access is a formality. 92% of teens aged 13–17 go online daily, and 24% of teens said that they are online "almost constantly."[10] Only 6% of teens said that they go online only once a week, and 2% reported going online less often than that.

Mobile devices facilitated this increase in teen access, with three-quarters of teens having access to a smartphone.[11] Although not all teens have access to data plans, many take advantage of WiFi at school, the library, or coffee shops. 91% of teens go online from their mobile devices at least occasionally, and 94% of teens who do go online from their mobile phone go online daily or more frequently. The spread of smartphone use is fairly consistent across lines of race/ethnicity: 85% of African American teens and 71% of both white and Hispanic teens have access to a smartphone.[12]

## Issues of Equity in Exposure to Informal Learning Opportunities

Even with an increase in digital access, issues of equity remain in terms of access to informal learning opportunities for many youth. A lack of this type of access can have lasting effects when it comes to what young people envision for their future. Examples of this are seen when looking at youth exposure to STEM activities in informal learning environments. A report released by the Girl Scouts of America indicates that girls who are interested in STEM and the potential of STEM careers are more likely to have participated in "hands-on science activities, gone to science/tech museums, and engaged in an extracurricular STEM activity."[13] This finding suggests that basic exposure can help teens realize entirely new interests and potential future career paths.

A report from the National Women's Law Center offers several suggestions to help eliminate this type of educational disparity. These include "increasing access to educational opportunities that promote diversity and reduce racial isolation" and "ensuring access to curricula that will help students build strong academic foundations . . . such as STEM courses and courses . . . that develop critical-thinking, reading, and math skills."[14] The report also states that schools need to "improve extracurricular opportunities and participation among African American girls" and to "improve STEM opportunities and achievement for African American girls."[15] This helps to make clear the importance of supporting interests in out-of-school learning environments, such as libraries, as a way to create opportunities for academic and future success.

## Disparities with Technology-Related Topics for Non-Dominant Populations

Lack of access to informal learning opportunities can foster gaps in diversity in certain fields, such as those related to STEM. Gaps persist in employment diversity for many computing and science jobs. Only 3% of African American women and 1% of Latinas hold computing jobs.[16] Only 5% of scientists and engineers working in science and engineering occupations are African American and only 6% are Hispanic.[17] This lack of representation in the workforce is potentially created by youth experiences that happen years earlier in school classrooms and informal learning environments.

Current research highlights the fact that despite attempts to address inequality through formal education, inequalities still exist. Gender and racial/ethnic disparities represent a stratification, which is troubling from a sociocultural and social justice perspective.[18] Women and girls from low-income families face more obstacles, which in turn reduces their career aspirations and expectations.[19] There is a consensus forming that starting in early adolescence, youth begin to think concretely about their futures, and these early thoughts impact how the youth prepare for their chosen career.[20] Existing research already describes the importance of exposure to disciplines that could potentially lead to future opportunities and career pathways.[21] This is a central reason as to why it is essential that youth have access to a variety of high-quality informal learning environments for their future career opportunities, as well as their larger learning ecology.

## Connecting Informal Learning to Other Settings

Even when youth have equitable opportunities for learning, many do not see the importance or value of the skills they use and learn in their interest spaces. Library staff have the opportunity to help teens make connections from informal learning to other settings. How librarians can do this is described in the rest of this chapter.

As mentioned earlier, exposure to a variety of experiences can have profound influence on youth interest and their approach to future opportunities and pathways. The connection between informal and formal learning can be seen as part of an ecology of learning in which people participate. A learning ecology is defined as "the set of contexts found in physical or virtual spaces that provide opportunities for learning."[22] An important part of the framework is that it links learning from one context to another or one person to another.[23] This framework elevates the idea that what youth do in their interest spaces is relevant and that this learning can connect to other settings. There are many contexts of learning that can impact youth, not just school, but community organizations: for example, after-school clubs, out-of-school organizations like the Girl Scouts, and informal learning programs like Girls Who Code. Viewing youth learning in this way provides the opportunity to look at the "learning lives" of young people not as points in time but connected across time.[24] This framework highlights the interconnectedness of the different parts of a youth's life in which they are learning.

King Beach uses the term "consequential transition" as a way to describe the connections that youth could potentially create between their informal and formal learning environments.[25] "Transitions are consequential when they are consciously reflected on, often struggled with, and the eventual outcome changes one's sense of self and social positioning."[26] This idea of transition is still somewhat limited and still rooted in the idea of transfer, so the idea of consequential connections has been used by certain scholars[27] as a way to describe the supports that foster connected civics. Consequential connections, as defined here, are mechanisms that support connections between young people's interests, peer culture, and academic level, which create opportunities for youth to have their expertise and knowledge valued and can potentially lead to future opportunities or career paths. Having access to technology is not enough; access to mentors and cultivated opportunities are needed as well. It is necessary for learners to have access to continual opportunities for positive experiences that offer up future trajectories.[28]

## Connected Learning

For nearly a decade, a growing body of research has explored young people's learning in their peer and leisure spaces. This research led to the development of a framework through which to view a youth learning ecology: connected learning.[29] Connected learning "advocates for broadened access to learning that is socially embedded, interest-driven, and oriented toward educational, economic, and political opportunity."[30] It is about bringing together peer and community support for interest- and passion-driven learning, and translating and linking that learning to academic success and eventually to career success. Although the agenda is not necessarily new, it is being approached in a new way. In the early part of the 20th century, John Dewey posed the idea of viewing education as seamless across all aspects of life.[31] For some youth, this seamless education is already a reality; however, for a majority of youth it is not. Fortunately, today's technology allows Dewey's vision to be more in reach than ever before, because technology can support inquiry-, interest-, and project-focused learning, as well as provide connections with those who have similar interests, for youth across all walks of life.

**Figure 2-1. Tips on Bringing Connected Learning to Libraries**

Connecting to Youth Interest

- Ask individual teens directly as one encounters them in practice what they are interested in.

- Build trusting relationships developed without judgment. Use casual conversation starters, such as commenting on book selections teens have made, asking about musical interests if they often wear headphones, and other such approaches based on contextual clues.

- Ask members of the teen advisory board or teen volunteers about their interests.

Supporting Peer-Supported Learning

- Have youth help design or run programs in which they have expertise, whether their interests are in book or video game clubs, fiber crafting, or computer programming.

- Allow programs to be flexible enough that peers are able to ask each other for feedback and advice.

- Library staff can position themselves as co-learners, instead of as pure experts, and be willing to try programming that they have not already mastered.

Fostering Production and Creation

- Programmatically, it is about offering a challenge that is open-ended, in which those participating have the option to choose their own product and create what they feel passionately about while seeking support when needed from those around them.

Access to technology alone is not enough; mentors and cultivated opportunities are needed as well. Learners need continual opportunities for positive experiences that add to or offer future trajectories.[32] Despite challenges that this type of learning approach presents, it is achievable and library staff are situated in the perfect place between school and home to help youth achieve it.

The research of the intersection of connected learning and libraries is nascent. Only a few articles touch on different implementations of connected learning in library contexts. Mimi Ito and Crystle Martin briefly discussed results from a month of webinars that described the relationship between connected learning and libraries.[33] An article by Åke Nygren suggests changes that librarians and library administrators need to make to their current practice.[34] It proposes that librarians build a transboundary network; reach out to the local community; host events of tinkering, learning, and making; and join a MOOC (massive open online course). Along with these guidelines, library managers need to empower their staff; stop digital environments that block learning; start a Hive network—a group comprised of organizations and individuals who want to create opportunities for youth to learn outside of school; and find partners in academia, the public sector, and industry.[35]

## Learning in Libraries

Libraries and library staff need to support connected learning by locating their efforts within a broader ecosystem of youth learning and by actively supporting connections to and from their programs and spaces. Libraries, which have long been centers of community activity, are uniquely situated to become a nexus of connected learning because their mission centers on personalized and interest-driven learning. As guides to information and technical literacy, library staff are often already guides to connected learning. Libraries are also perceived in highly favorable ways by non-dominant populations as lifelines to learning, technology, and information. A recent Pew Internet and American Life study indicates that African American and Latino families are more likely than their white and Asian counterparts to place a high value on libraries.[36] Libraries are well positioned to not only connect formal and informal learning, but also to do this for the populations that are most marginalized in terms of traditional academic programs and indicators.

## Examples of Librarians and Library Staff Supporting Youth Learning

What can it look like when library staff support youth learning? The examples from a variety of library settings help to answer that question.

# A Rural Library

At a rural library in Washington State, Samantha, a teen librarian, works to introduce teens to new ideas and interests, through informal learning, with potential for helping teens learn about career pathways. One example is a STEAM program that Samantha designed. For each day of the week, she creates a program for each letter of STEAM (Science, Technology, Engineering, Art, and Math). Previously, Samantha conducted an art and science program, but was feeling a little intimidated by this expansion to her program. Samantha decided that she could either try something completely new or use an existing program she was familiar with. For example, Samantha had used Rovers—small Arduino-based robots that can be programmed by youth and then operated using the youth-created programming—and could build on the activity. She also connected more intentionally with parents and caregivers as a way to draw on their personal professional expertise.

The STEAM program was a success, and as the program grew Samantha developed opportunities for teen mentorship. She fostered relationships with teens and was then able to help them develop leadership skills. Samantha's process included going through a project plan with teens and then giving them the chance demonstrate the activity to other participants in the program.

Not only was Samantha helping teens gain leadership skills; she supported acquisition of 21st-century skills and computational thinking by providing opportunities for all involved to problem solve, iterate, and learn by trial and error. This approach clearly supported collaborative and peer learning.

For Samantha, creating this new series of programming was a rewarding experience. She notes that facilitating these programs taught her to experiment. Revising plans along the way is a necessity. She had originally planned to run the program every week but pared it down to six times a semester. Samantha warns that not everything is going to go as planned, but this is to be expected.

This type of programming was new for Samantha. Before designing this series, her philosophy of library programs centered on the idea that "learning was not the role of libraries." Samantha goes on to say, "[That was] until STEAM programming [came along]." Samantha explains,

"STEAM lends itself to informal learning; [it] might be the kind of thing kids could do in their home already, but many don't. The family kind of learning that some families can't/don't do because of lack of resources, time, etc. There are many young families in my community with not a lot of money and not a lot of options. The library's role is to provide and facilitate learning opportunities outside of school. It is supplementary. Things that they wouldn't get in school."

Samantha also stresses the importance of offering teens real work experience, as she was able to provide in her STEAM programs. Leadership experiences in libraries, she says, "teach them about being on time, calling in when sick, structuring volunteering like a real job to give them that experience and possibly a leg up in the future." Actual coaching and mentoring became part of her programming; the teens needed feedback on their actions. She feels that it was easy to build into current programs, and that it was value added for the programs and the teens. She concludes that a lot of libraries are reluctant to implement STEAM programming. They are afraid of not being an expert. She points out, "You can make valuable experiences for kids and teens without being an expert."

## Urban Library: Teen-Only Space

As a teen librarian in a southern urban library serving mostly African American youth, Juliette makes teen programming an important part of her practice. She offers one program a day, ranging from small programs like self-directed trivia questions to a large program once a month. These programs not only teach teens life skills but often impact youth outside of the library experience.

For example, Juliette offers programs that teach life skills and career preparation. The Kitchen Chemistry program fits into this category. Once a month, teens come to explore the intersection of food and chemistry. This program not only teaches youth the important skill of cooking, but also about the chemistry behind cooking. Juliette's Teen Fashion Apprentice program is an opportunity for youth interested in fashion to explore it as a career. She partnered with local community members who work in fashion and with institutions that provide hair and makeup training. These professionals come to the library to talk with teens, who are then offered the chance to have an internship working with a professional in their studio to learn about the day-to-day work of a fashion career. These programs not only support career readiness; they also help develop lifelong learning skills from cooking to interviewing.

Juliette has a strong belief about the steps required to design programs of this type. First, she views her library as a "destination library." She works to create an environment where youth feel welcome and want to hang out. This means she needs things for them to do. When designing programs, she focuses on meeting teens where they are. "You may have an idea of what teens would be interested in, but you have to understand that when teens are ready, they will take something in but it can't be forced." For her, it is about "creating lifelong learners." She says the most important part of her practice is "developing relationships so we can serve [teens] again wherever they are at as they go through life." She continues, "Learning is a two-way street. If we aren't learning from them, we aren't serving them well. You need to be flexible, be willing to shift roles and see it more like a community space, and support learning as a network."

## Urban Library: Teen Media Space

Hyun, a teen librarian, runs a tech-driven media space in a library that shares a building with a high school. She creates opportunities for youth to lead interest-driven technology-based programs. Examples include a teen who organized a reception for a photography exhibit and another teen who organized a film screening. By organizing these events, the teens were able to explore what it means to be an artist, learning what it takes to create, promote, and exhibit work—all aspects of informal learning.

The teen librarian brokered a connection between an intern who wanted to be a photographer and a professional wedding photographer. Hyun set the intern up with an informational interview, giving the teen the opportunity to ask the professional about starting and maintaining a photography business. Working as an informal learning mentor, the librarian was able to leverage the intern's interest in photography into a professional opportunity where the teen could better understand what it is like to have a career in photography.

Hyun runs an internship through the lens of connected learning (CL). "I can practice CL because I've had the chance to get to know the interns so well. I know what their goals and strengths are, so I actively try to find resources that match those. . . . [For example, I] encouraged [one of my interns] to lead the workshop and advocate for the [Media Space]. Another intern wants to be a doctor, so I had him do the tutoring and other workshops so he could practice his communication and presentation skills. Another is interested in photography; she took photos of staff members at work, and another intern interviewed each staff member and selected the best representatives for the project they were working on. [The teen photographer] took about 100 photos of each staff member. It was good for her because she got to work with people she had never met before, unlike previous photos she had taken that had mostly been of friends. It gave her the experience of working with clients and taking portraiture. The interns went through the library to photograph and interview library workers. After interviewing 15 librarians for three hours a week, they gained a good idea of how varied librarianship can be."

## Branch Library, Urban System

Carol is a teen librarian with 23 years of experience working in a largely low-income Latino immigrant community. At the urban branch library where she works, Carol offers programs that focus on helping youth who come from non-English-speaking households to prepare for the future. The teens she serves face unique challenges, including being the first in their families to consider attending college. Along with challenges related to being a first-generation college student, these students also face challenges related to documentation status.

To help the teens she serves navigate the complicated world of college readiness, Carol created a set of programs. First, she annually holds a five-week SAT study course. In week one, the teens take a practice test. For the following weeks, based on the results of the practice test, the teens have study sessions on how to improve their work in the English, math, and essay sections. At week five, the teens take the test again. The program has been very successful. The room can only seat 70, but usually more than 100 sign up for the program.

Carol also holds workshops for college preparation. This includes a workshop for parents and students on financial aid, including conversation about deadlines. She offers workshops on study habits and time management. Another program Carol hosts is a panel made up of previous volunteers who have gone to college and high school students who are applying to college. These youth are generally all first-generation college students and come from an area where going to college is far from being a given. The students on the panel talk about their experience with everything from filling out college applications and FAFSA to understanding financial aid packages and choosing a major. The panel creates an opportunity for candid information sharing and dialogue between college students and those considering going to college. The panelists often talked about how working at the library had an impact on their ability to envision college being within their reach and how Carol's mentorship allowing them to develop their interest in tech (through programs like teen-organized tech-petting zoos) helped them envision potential career opportunities.

Carol also has a very active volunteer program. All volunteers are required to apply for the program, and when accepted, one of the assigned tasks is to help run programs. "The way I approach the volunteers and their training and how I work with them is that I am very conscious that I am building their confidence and skills. And I tell them that. I give them a lot of responsibility and decision-making ability. I tell them they are a team. I give them a job to do immediately. I will have them set up the room in a certain way as a group and then leave. Depending on the group, they've either pulled together as a team and done it or are standing around. If they haven't set up the room, I give it to them again. Usually the second time they figure it out. If I have a volunteer helping a student on the computer who tells me a problem, I ask them, 'How do you think you can solve it?' I use the Socratic method a lot. Afterward I tell them very specifically 'that was really good leadership' or 'that was really good problem solving.' People forget how important feedback is—all people want to see their work valued. If a teen is showing natural leadership, I will put them in charge of something and then direct other teens to that teen. I will also encourage a teen who is hanging back to take leadership. With a teen who was acting immaturely, I had a conversation about his leadership and overall approach. I want these teens to see that they are running these programs and running the library. I want them to see they have these skills and can do it."

Carol continues, "Teens have the opportunity to become my administrative assistant. They are learning real life skills. One teen who had been working as my admin then got a job in an eyeglass lab as a senior because she had developed a lot of confidence working in the library. The teens learn a lot of problem-solving skills from the work." She says, "I've written so many recommendations for teens over the years that help them on their journey." Carol has an approach that supports the learning of the teens. She explains that she supports her teens "whether it is fixing [a] car, learning to canoe, finding a job, or finding relief from domestic abuse."

Connected learning is a framework under constant development that offers principles and examples that can be adapted and remixed. Putting connected learning into practice provides a lot of opportunities for libraries and the teens they serve. Integrating the framework into library service can start as a small addition to an existing program and lead to a complete redesign of the way a library supports informal learning.

# Conclusion

Supporting youth learning is essential to youth success. For youth, learning is not something that happens only in the six hours a day they are in school, but instead their learning expands beyond their formal learning environments into out-of-school locations such as the public library. The learning that teens participate in outside of their formal learning environment offers opportunities for them to expand their horizons.

Librarians need to bring connected learning into their practice and into their library. This can necessitate changes in approach and priorities, but as the examples included in this chapter illustrate, implementing connected learning does not require money—it requires a certain mindset. It is about creating relationships with teens and creating opportunities for youth to be exposed to and pursue interests, to leverage peer learning, and to connect interest to opportunity—all of these in turn support youth career and college readiness. Connected learning is not just a way to describe learning that is happening in interest spaces; it is also a model for design, intervention, and policy. It is at the intersections of youth learning where librarians have the opportunity for the largest impact. Connected learning is not about a technology or a technique; it is about focusing the learning on the learner.

# Notes

1. Constance Steinkuehler, "Massively Multiplayer Online Gaming as a Constellation of Literacy Practices," *E-Learning and Digital Media* 4, no. 3 (2007): 297–318, doi:10.2304/elea.2007.4.3.297; Constance Steinkuehler and Elizabeth King, "Digital Literacies for the Disengaged: Creating After School Contexts to Support Boys' Game-Based Literacy Skills," *On the Horizon* 17, no. 1 (2009): 47–59, doi:10.1108/10748120910936144; Crystle Martin, *Voyage Across a Constellation of Information: Information Literacy in Interest-Driven Learning Communities* (New York: Peter Lang, 2014).

2. Steinkuehler, "Massively Multiplayer Online Gaming."

3. Martin, *Voyage Across a Constellation of Information.*

4. Rebecca W. Black, *Adolescents and Online Fan Fiction* (New York: Lang, 2008).

5. Constance Steinkuehler and Caroline C. Williams, "Math as Narrative in WoW Forum Discussions," *International Journal of Learning and Media* 1, no. 3 (2009), doi:10.1162/ijlm_a_00028.

6. Amanda Ochsner, "Typically Untypical Affinity Practices Making a Mass Effect" (master's thesis, University of Wisconsin, Madison, 2012).

7. John Seely Brown, Allan Collins, and Paul Duguid, "Situated Cognition and the Culture of Learning," *Educational Researcher* 18, no. 1 (1989): 32, doi:10.2307/1176008.

8. Rachel Cody Pfister, *Hats for House Elves: Connected Learning and Civic Engagement in Hogwarts at Ravelry* (Digital Media and Learning Research Hub, May 15, 2014), http://clrn.dmlhub.net/wp-content/uploads/2014/05/hatsfor-houseelves.pdf (accessed February 22, 2017).

9. Karen Brennan, Andre Monroy-Hernandez, and Mitchel Resnick, "Making Projects, Making Friends: Online Community as Catalyst for Interactive Media Creation," *New Directions for Youth Development*, no. 128 (2010): 75–83, doi:10.1002/yd.377.

10. Amanda Lenhart, *Teens, Social Media, and Technology Overview 2015* (Pew Research Center, April 2015), http://www.pewinternet.org/files/2015/04/PI_TeensandTech_Update2015_0409151.pdf (accessed February 22, 2017).

11. Ibid.

12. Ibid.

13. Kamla Modi, Judy Schoenberg, and Kimberlee Salmond, *Generation STEM: What Girls Say about Science, Technology, Engineering, and Math* (Girl Scout Research Institute, 2012), http://www.girlscouts.org/content/dam/girlscouts-gsusa/forms-and-documents/about-girl-scouts/research/generation_stem_full_report.pdf (accessed February 22, 2017).

14. NAACP Legal Defense and Educational Fund and the National Women's Law Center, *Unlocking Opportunity for African American Girls: A Call to Action for Educational Equity* (2014), http://www.nwlc.org/sites/default/files/pdfs/unlocking_opportunity_for_african_american_girls_final.pdf (accessed February 22, 2017).

15. Ibid., 43.

16. Catherine Ashcraft, Brad McLain, and Elizabeth Eger, *Women in Tech: The Facts, 2016 Update* (National Center for Women and Information Technology, 2015), https://www.ncwit.org/sites/default/files/resources/ncwit_women-in-it_2016-full-report_final-web06012016.pdf (accessed February 22, 2017).

17. National Center for Science and Engineering Statistics, *Women, Minorities, and Persons with Disabilities in Science and Engineering* (2017), https://www.nsf.gov/statistics/2017/nsf17310/ (accessed February 22, 2017.).

18. C. Riegle-Crumb and B. King, "Questioning a White Male Advantage in STEM: Examining Disparities in College Major by Gender and Race/Ethnicity," *Educational Researcher* 39, no. 9 (2010): 656–64, doi:10.3102/0013189x10391657.

19. Desirae M. Domenico and Karen H. Jones, "Career Aspirations of Women in the 20th Century," *Journal of Career and Technical Education* 22, no. 2 (2007), doi:10.21061/jcte.v22i2.430; Yacoub Khallad, "Education and Career Aspirations of Palestinian and U.S. Youth," *Journal of Social Psychology* 140, no. 6 (2000): 789–91, doi:10.1080/00224540009600517; Thomas Voglia, "Gender Equity Issues in CTE and STEM Education," *Tech Directions* 72, no. 7 (2013): 14; Cary M. Watson, Teri Quatman, and Erik Edler, "Career Aspirations of Adolescent Girls: Effects of Achievement Level, Grade, and Single-Sex School Environment," *Sex Roles* 46, nos. 9/10 (2002): 323–35, doi:10.1023/a:1020228613796.

20. Richard W. Auger, Anne E. Blackhurst, and Kay Herting Wahl, "The Development of Elementary-Aged Children's Career Aspirations and Expectations," *Professional School Counseling* 8, no. 4 (2005): 322–29, http://www.jstor.org/stable/42732626; Albert Bandura, Claudio Barbaranelli, Gian Vittorio Caprara, and Concetta Pastorelli, "Self-Efficacy Beliefs as Shapers of Children's Aspirations and Career Trajectories," *Child Development* 72, no. 1 (2001): 187–206, http://www.jstor.org/stable/1132479; Catherine Riegle-Crumb, Chelsea Moore, and Aida Ramos-Wada, "Who Wants to Have a Career in Science or Math? Exploring Adolescents' Future Aspirations by Gender and Race/Ethnicity," *Science Education* 95, no. 3 (2010): 458–76, doi:10.1002/sce.20431.

21. National Resource Council, *Successful K–12 STEM Education: Identifying Effective Approaches in Science, Technology, Engineering, and Mathematics* (Washington, DC: National Academies Press, 2011); Modi, Schoenberg, and Salmond, *Generation STEM*.

22. Brigid Barron, "Learning Ecologies for Technological Fluency: Gender and Experience Differences," *Journal of Educational Computing Research* 31,

no. 1 (2004): 1–36, doi:10.2190/1n20-vv12-4rb5-33va; Brigid Barron, "Interest and Self-Sustained Learning as Catalysts of Development: A Learning Ecology Perspective," *Human Development* 49, no. 4 (2006): 193–224, doi:10.1159/000094368.

23. Barron, "Interest and Self-Sustained Learning."

24. Ola Erstad, "Digital Disconnect? The 'Digital Learner' and the School," in *Identity, Community, and Learning Lives in the Digital Age*, ed. J. Sefton Green (Cambridge: Cambridge University Press, 2012), 87–106.

25. King Beach, "Consequential Transitions: A Sociocultural Expedition Beyond Transfer in Education," *Review of Research in Education* 24 (1999): 101–39, doi:10.2307/1167268.

26. Ibid., 114.

27. Mizuko Ito, Elisabeth Soep, Neta Kligler-Vilenchik, Sangita Shresthova, Liana Gamber-Thompson, and Arely Zimmerman, "Learning Connected Civics: Narratives, Practices, Infrastructures," *Curriculum Inquiry* 45, no. 1 (2015): 10–29, doi:10.1080/03626784.2014.995063.

28. June Ahn, Mega Subramaniam, Elizabeth Bonsignore, Anthony Pellicone, Amanda Waugh, and Jason Yip, "'I Want to Be a Game Designer or Scientist': Connected Learning and Developing Identities with Urban, African-American Youth," *Proceedings of the Eleventh International Conference of the Learning Sciences* (2014), http://ahnjune.com/wp-content/uploads/2014/04/ICLS2014-Sci-Dentity-camera-ready.pdf (accessed February 22, 2017).

29. Barron, "Learning Ecologies for Technological Fluency"; Barron, "Interest and Self-Sustained Learning."

30. Mizuko Ito, Kris Gutiérrez, Sonia Livingstone, Bill Penuel, Jean Rhodes, Katie Salen, Juliet Schor, Julian Sefton-Green, and S. Craig Watkins, *Connected Learning: An Agenda for Research and Design* (Digital Media and Learning Research Hub, January 2013), http://dmlhub.net/wp-content/uploads/files/Connected_Learning_report.pdf (accessed February 22, 2017).

31. John Dewey, *Education and Experience* (New York: Macmillan, 1938).

32. Ahn et al., "'I Want to Be a Game Designer or Scientist.'"

33. Mizuko Ito and Crystle Martin, "Connected Learning and the Future of Libraries," *Young Adult Library Services (YALS)*, 12, no. 1 (2013): 29–32.

34. Åke Nygren, "Conference Resource Papers," *Federal Sentencing Reporter* 15, no. 3, Federal Sentencing Guidelines Symposium (February 1, 2003): 191–214, http://library.ifla.org/1014/1/167-nygren-en.pdf (accessed February 22, 2017).

35. Mark Bilandzic, "Connected Learning in the Library as a Product of Hacking, Making, Social Diversity and Messiness," *Interactive Learning Environments* 24, no. 1 (2013): 158–77, doi:10.1080/10494820.2013.825811 (accessed Feb-

ruary 22, 2017).

36. John Horrigan, *Libraries at the Crossroads* (Pew Research Center, September 15, 2015), http://www.pewinternet.org/files/2015/09/2015-09-15_libraries_FINAL.pdf (accessed February 22, 2017).

## JOHNSON COUNTY LIBRARY
# Digital Storytelling

### KATE PICKETT & MEGAN MASCORRO-JACKSON

## What Did You Want to Achieve?

We had several educational objectives. We focused on helping students to

- Explore telling their own stories using their own voice.

- Gain an understanding of the language used by Shakespeare. If you can gain command over language, you can do anything.

- Experience theater as a vehicle for social change, and learn to be agents for their own change.

- See connections in storytelling from Shakespeare to modern writing for stage and screen.

- Create digital stories to keep as evidence of skills learned.

- Write a monologue to keep as evidence of skills learned.

- Attend a play at a regional theater with an opportunity to provide feedback and ask questions of playwright and actors after the show.

## Overview of the Program/Project

In a partnership between Olathe School District, the Kansas City Repertory Theater, and the Johnson County Library, we offered a seven-week course for students at the Foundations juvenile detention center. The course gave students the chance to explore storytelling in multiple forms from the printed word to live theater production. Students explored Shakespeare, saw a performance of *Sticky Traps*—the most recent play by playwright Nathan Jackson—and investigated a variety of modern storytelling techniques. Participants learned to express themselves, understand the value of a story and words, and had the opportunity to become agents for change in their community.

## What Challenges Did You Face and How Did You Overcome Them?

Probably the biggest challenge was bringing technology into a secure facility. Luckily, we didn't have to fight much of the sometimes common battle related to the potential for metal laptops to be used as weapons. The school purchased laptops earlier in the year, so they were on site already. However, detention center staff were very concerned about students being able to access the Internet. We worked out a compromise where the laptops were locked down with as much security as possible. We also promised that library staff would be with the students and laptops at all times: at no time would we allow students to use the laptops unsupervised. Also, because of the fluctuating nature of their population, we needed to make each piece of the project easy to consume, so someone could easily jump in on the project and not feel like they couldn't catch up. We had 5–8 new students over the course of the seven-week unit.

## What Did You Learn?

We learned a lot. First, orchestrating a program with multiple partners is tough! If we thought managing a library schedule was difficult, try managing to work with theater staff, public school teachers, and corrections staff so as to achieve one goal—sometimes communication felt futile. But it all turned out well and ultimately brought a richer experience to the students.

We learned that we didn't know as much as we thought we did. We went in feeling pretty comfortable with podcasting and stop-motion animation, but ultimately, by giving students time to mess around and show us what they discovered, we learned more from them than we would ever have been able to teach.

And we learned that project-based, interest-driven learning takes a lot of time. We had to dedicate a lot of staff time to making the tools available to students (since as I mentioned before we couldn't leave the students alone with the laptops). For a public library that (like many others) is strapped for capacity, it was a big investment, but it really paid off.

## How Does This Work Connect to YALSA's Futures Report and Vision?

This project is connected to several components of the Futures Report. These include

- A focus on multiple literacies. Students engaged with this project were able to improve skills in digital and print-based literacies.

- Giving students the opportunity to engage in real-life experiences through interaction with a playwright and actors.

- Developing relationships and partnerships with multiple community agencies. Through our work with a local school district, a juvenile detention center, and a theater, we were able to support the academic and personal interest needs of youth.

BOSTON (MA) PUBLIC LIBRARY

# A New Vision for a New Teen Space

JESSI SNOW

## What Did You Want to Achieve?

To create a space, now called Teen Central, that reflects the interests and needs of teens in the community. We worked to create a space with a focus on HOMAGO; for hanging out (lots of chairs and couches), messing around (a gaming lounge with three gaming systems for teens to access and consume games/media, programs to participate in, and to mess around with) and geeking out (the Lab, a digital makerspace for teens to create, learn, and collaborate).

## Overview of the Program/Project

A year before the new space opened, we worked to outline the vision of the space. We started by building a survey that teens completed as a way to help us shape programming.

The survey was given to teens a year before the new space opened, and they were asked how, why, and when they use the Central Library. We

also asked them to rank in order of importance and interest the type of programs they were interested in participating in, including the following: college readiness, job readiness (résumé workshops, interview skills), music creation, technology (3-D creation, engineering, music creation, coding, etc.), craft programs, and teen leadership programs. The programs that were ranked the highest were job readiness, college preparedness, and technology programming.

The space opened in February 2015, and since its opening, teen engagement at the Central Library has skyrocketed.

## What Challenges Did You Face and How Did You Overcome Them?

None of this happened overnight or even in just a year. It's taken time and continues to take time. One of the big challenges has been in defining the Lab (digital makerspace) and really having teens understand the intent of the space and then use it as intended. We focus programs in the Lab based on the research from the Futures Report and from direct input from teens. We identified some innovative programs that teens have expressed interest in, developed a curriculum of programs based on the Futures Report, and continue to bring in outside organizations of professionals and organizations that specialize in coding, music creation, graphic design, 3-D design and making; however, we haven't really been reaching those teens who need and want this type of program. We are really trying to connect with outside organizations and schools that work with underserved teens to try identify their needs for technology programs and then develop a curriculum that works to support

those needs. We are looking at different ways to try to serve those who need it, whether it's in the library or outside the walls of the library.

## What Did You Learn?

We completely rethought how we present our programs and now think about them in ways so that they address introducing teens to twenty-first-century digital literacy skills, provide them with exposure to possible careers, and introduce them to actual careers. We are working more closely with community partners in order to achieve this. And we make sure to talk with teens about ways in which skills learned are transferable and the ways they can include them in their résumés and in job interviews.

## How Does This Work Connect to YALSA's Futures Report and Vision?

All of the staff in Teen Central were asked to read the YALSA Futures Report on their own and then met as a team to discuss areas of importance and pieces to focus on for Teen Central. As a result we now focus on these Futures-related areas:

- Programming based on input from teens and a connected-learning focus.

- Outreach that is consistent, deliberate, and purposeful.

- Programs that focus on career readiness.

# CHAPTER 3

# Working Together: Youth-Adult Partnerships to Enhance Youth Voice

JUAN RUBIO

Authentic education is not carried on by "A" for "B" or by "A" about "B," but rather by "A" *with* "B" mediated by the world, a world that impresses and challenges both parties, giving rise to opinions about it.

—Paulo Freire, *Pedagogy of the Oppressed* (2014)[1]

## Introduction

In 2016, approximately 50 million students were enrolled in a public school in the United States,[2] and around 10 million participated in an after-school program, an increase of 15% from 2009.[3] With the large number of youth attending formal and informal learning programs in the United States, the opportunities for adults to have an impact on how young people learn is extraordinary. With this opportunity in mind, now is the time to view learning environments as social spaces where adults and young people bring a set of social norms with them. Understanding what these social norms are and how they can affect youth-adult partnerships in learning spaces is critical when incorporating youth voice in learning programs. Identifying dynamics created by the different set of norms a student brings to a place of learning helps build better engagement and leads to enhanced youth voice.

Since learning spaces are governed by relationships with social dynamics and power relationships and shaped by cultural-historical experiences, working for increased youth voice within such a structure will move learning outcomes toward a more inclusive experience for both teens and adults.

Within library spaces, library staff working with teens should adopt a youth voice model: a model in which adults and teens work together on decision making, planning, and implementation. This model provides youth with real opportunities for having a voice in what happens in library programs and services, which is essential in developing and implementing successful programs for teens. By establishing strong youth-adult social relationships through youth voice, it's possible to offer programs rooted in youth self-expression and cultural and social awareness, which helps develop agency in youth and move toward a more equitable form of learning.

This chapter discusses youth voice and explores several aspects of the framework of using youth voice:

- Why including youth voice in learning programs is important.

- Strategies for adult facilitators on how to design programs with a strong youth voice.

- Promoting youth voice as a pathway to avoid the reproduction of social inequalities in learning environments and case studies.

- Successful application of youth voice in teen library services.

In particular, the chapter focuses on and provides examples of the use of digital media programs as a way to include youth voice. These present a unique opportunity to embed youth voice in the library learning experience.

## What Is Youth Voice?

Youth voice is broadly defined as "the perception that one's opinions are heard and respected by others particularly adults."[4] Sara Vogel is a research assistant and PhD student for Global Education at the Graduate Center of the City University of New York, who has many years of experience working as an educator. She explains how youth voice can be twofold: (1) youth express their idea of the world, and (2) youth express opinions on what and how they are learning. "The learning can take different forms: their opinions about things, their self-expression, their message to the world. What the projects are allowing them to say about the world. It can also extend to which input they have on what they learn, their autonomy in the learning process,"[5] Vogel notes. Although this refers more to the way that youth voice their opinions during the learning process, it provides a starting point to begin working toward programs that include strong youth voice in them.

## Why Youth Voice Is Important

In teen library programs, adults take over the process while facilitating learning. For example, teens are told what resources to use, what the final goal is, and even how to achieve that goal. Sometimes this approach is used simply because it's easier. Incorporating youth voice takes time, and including teens in a process as active learners requires a higher degree of effort and preparation from the adult than an entirely adult-led/adult-voice experience. Guiding teens through the creative process, analyzing situations, or synthesizing ideas is time-consuming and not easy to successfully accomplish. However, if the time is taken to incorporate youth voice into the learning, the results are far more fulfilling for both the teens and adults. Adults have greater opportunities for professional satisfaction if a program gives teens the platform to develop skills that will shape their future. Unless learning institutions such as libraries begin to incorporate youth voice as an integral part of their offerings, youth and especially minority youth will continue consuming and producing media that frequently has nothing to do with how they conceive of their world and their community.

## An Adult Who Doesn't Disappear from the Room

"Youth voice" or "student voice" has been part of recent academic conversation. When educators talk about youth voice, they often refer to listening to the opinions of youth. More recently, this focus has been

## Figure 3-1. Case 1: The Case of the Missing Pages— Helping Students Move Forward

I was running a program with the Brooklyn Public Library in which teens designed a geo-locative game. (A geo-locative game is one in which the player's location is used in the game play such as with Pokémon Go.) The game was about a ghost that haunted the library. The teens had a lot of ideas: alternate endings, decoys, the ways in which the paths a player took would change depending on random choices within the game. In developing the game the teens were inspired by a tour of the library's stacks housed in the basement.

The program used a game design studio format. Within that format, teens joined a group based on their own personal interests: storytelling, research, programming, play-testing. Teams decided who would be the project manager based on pitches made by those interested in taking on that role.

The project manager was in charge of keeping the groups on task for the ten weeks we had to design and develop the game. I planned the program carefully, making sure to cover all the content with enough time to have a game ready by the end of the program. I did end up in a difficult position: the teens needed help shaping their game. The key elements (core game idea, game goal, game story, characters, rules, location) were in place, but they were not well organized. We brainstormed for almost two hours. The teens seemed defeated at the end; they were confused and not sure how the program would move forward. Could we complete the program in time? Would the game be ready for others to play at the end of the ten weeks?

I went home and created a sort of "mood board" with all the ideas that the teens had talked about. I felt better: all the pieces were there. (The board is available at https://realtimeboard.com/app/board/iX-jVOfhALJc=/.) The story had an arc, some mechanics, and elements that linked the game to the location. I was a bit hesitant to present the mood board to the teens the next day. Did I interfere too much with their design? Was I taking over their creative process?

I started the session the next day by telling the teens I had organized their ideas and put them together in a way that connected them all.

Then I showed them the board. To my surprise, they were very pleased and relieved. They told me they were afraid their game would not be ready on time for the final capstone event. The project manager was really happy and came to tell me it was so helpful to see the game more developed. After that, the students worked really hard and were very involved in creating the game. An extra session was added in the middle of the week to complete the game, and many students attended. We had a game to play at the end of the ten weeks: The Case of the Missing Pages.

This was a situation in which the adult intervention was much needed for the successful completion of the program. Youth did not explicitly ask for the intervention from the adult, but when it was done, they were pleased and were able to move ahead to the next phase of the design: fleshing out the story, programming, testing, and debugging it.

The adult must be aware of the progress being made. If at times the program has come to a stop, the facilitator should intervene and make adjustments to their ideas. If such intervention doesn't happen, teens might lose interest, and the program will not move ahead. If the concern for not stepping in is one related to including youth voice, providers should keep in mind there are many opportunities down the road where youth voice can come through, and that sometimes such interventions are needed.

Before this program, every time I heard someone mention youth voice in learning spaces, I imagined a group of young people providing ideas to create projects and the adult disappearing in the background, acting as a ghost with nothing to contribute. I used to advise coworkers to let the kids provide all the content for a program. After many years of experience working with youth on creating games, interactive narratives, and other media projects where creativity takes center stage, I have come to better understand the role of the adult in creating a strong youth voice and the critical role the adult has in enhancing that voice.

The adult has an active role when developing learning experiences for youth, by guiding teens' thought process as they engage in the creation of media and digital media programs.

identified as presenting a problem because it creates a construct that seemingly excludes adult voice in the learning experience. For this reason, scholars have proposed a shift from using the phrase and construct of "youth voice" to using that of "youth-adult partnerships." Rachel Bolstad writes:

> For many of us, the most problematic issue is that "student voice" approaches may not address underlying power differences between young people and adults—particularly in contexts such as schools where adult and youth roles are already tightly framed and the power differentials between adults and young people are deeply embedded. The idea of "listening to students" or "consulting young people" (including in non-educational settings, e.g., local government) is similarly critiqued for its potential to limit young people's involvement to providing a point of view or perspective, with no guarantee that their input will be taken into account or that they will have input into subsequent decisions.[6]

Earlier in my career, I thought enhancing youth voice meant that the adult should not say anything, that I would fade into the background and let the young people do all the work. However, based on my practice over the years, I discovered that adults can have a greater impact on youth voice if they are involved in the learning alongside of teens. Adults can develop partnerships with young people to create an environment that encourages sharing ideas, questioning decisions, helping with iteration, participating in brainstorming, and so on.

Bolstad proposes a new way of thinking about youth voice. "Lately I've become interested in the term youth-adult partnerships as an alternative to student voice,"[7] she writes. Youth-adult partnerships are described by Dana Mitra as "relationships in which both youth and adults have the potential to contribute to decision-making processes, to learn from one another, and to promote change."[8]

There are times when young people need more adult support to move things forward. "The Case of the Missing Pages" (see fig. 3-1) is a good example of this. As the adult, I stepped in to move the project forward to the next stage. When this is done in an environment of true youth voice where positive relationships are in place, young people will see the adult involvement not as an intrusion in the development of their project but rather as much-needed help. Youth should see the adult as an equal partner who is invested in the project. Seeing this involvement creates greater engagement as teens view the adult as an active and engaged participant in the process.

# Youth Voice Takes Different Forms

Identifying categories and levels of engagement from teens to achieve voice while learning helps in the design of programs that involve meaningful youth-adult partnerships. In some cases, youth voice is expressed in the production of media. Other times, their voice is one of civic engagement, taking action and proposing changes in policies affecting youth lives or communities. For instance, teens who are part of a video production program can decide what topic they are interested in and create a video in which that interest is front and center and even the topic of the video. This is youth voice in the form of media creation. Another example is when teens analyze a problem in their community, such as road conditions or dangerous intersections in proximity to their school. They then create awareness about an issue by bringing attention to the problem, creating a petition, and ultimately making change by taking the issue to their local government. Their voice thus becomes one of activism and civic engagement.

Institutional, staffing, and/or community requirements have an impact on what form of youth voice an activity takes. It's important from the beginning for the facilitator to identify the level of engagement that youth are able to have in the program. Designing and completing a game, for example, is a rather complex project, requiring many steps: conceiving the idea, creating a prototype to test the feasibility of the game, writing the game story, choosing characters, determining the goal of the game, developing the game in the platform of choice, play-testing, and so on. If the amount of time—number of weeks and/or hours—is not enough for participants to be part of all of the steps in the process, facilitators need to know that ahead of time complete some of those tasks themselves. For example, the facilitator could work with the students in the development of the game idea and story, leaving the development of the game as the responsibility of the facilitator.

The facilitator should be aware of challenges that can arise in the program. Working with teens of different age groups (younger and older teens together) can be challenging especially when working in a highly collaborative environment. Youth at different stages of development can differ drastically from their peers, and it might be hard to synthesize ideas and agree upon them. Having a clear plan for the program and how to include youth voice in it enable opportunities for achieving a satisfactory level of youth voice inclusion. No matter what format and level of inclusion youth voice takes, it's imperative for the adult facilitator to let teens know in what areas their voice will be included and why there are limitations in some instances.

It's also important to consider the outcomes of a program that incorporates youth voice. Bolstad lists the following frameworks for youth voice integration:

- *Constructivist learning:* The focus when integrating constructivist learning is on youth actively building their own meaning from learning experiences. Learning facilitators using constructivist-learning approaches should focus on the need to hear youth "voice," the teens' own views on their learning, in order for learning facilitators to identify and support next learning steps.

- *Inquiry learning approaches:* In these experiences, the "voice" of youth is elicited to identify and provide opportunities to pursue questions that interest them and, in the best examples, link meaningfully to teen lives beyond school.

- *Learning goal setting:* These outcomes relate to the development of youth leadership skills by incorporating youth voice in forums for decision making on various civic engagement–focused matters.

- *Psychological theories of personal development:* These are opportunities in which youth are encouraged to express their voice in order to increase their self-awareness and the ability to regulate their own behavior and thinking.

- *Diversity-based goal setting:* These outcomes acknowledge the rights of all youth to be engaged by and have a voice in their learning, regardless of their different individual starting points and any special learning needs and different "worldviews" associated with different backgrounds, cultures, and experiences.[9]

Whether young people are actively building their own meaning, identifying questions linked to their lives, or expressing different worldviews, it is a library staff member's role to design a program that provides the foundation to foster youth voice, which will lead to these kinds of deep participation.

# Digital Media as a Way to Bring Youth Voice to the Foreground

The immediate feedback that digital media provides can give teens the opportunity to see their ideas quickly come to life. When youth have an idea and are able to move from concept to realized project—whether it's a photo collage, a soundtrack, a game, or a computer program—they are likely to be engaged in the entire process. Teens create a product and want to share it with their friends, family, and mentors.

Incorporating the use of online tools and digital media provides youth with a way to connect to the content, bringing a familiar form of engagement to the learning and giving teens the opportunity of self-expression. As described by Mizuko Ito and colleagues, "Through digital media, youth today have countless accessible opportunities to share, create, and expand their horizons. They can access a wealth of knowledge as well as be participants, makers, and doers engaged in active and self-directed inquiry. The most activated and well-supported learners are using today's social, interactive, and online media to boost their learning and opportunity, attesting to the tremendous potential of new media for advancing learning."[10]

As learning providers create spaces for young people to include a strong youth voice component, close attention should be given to the tool by which such voice will be enhanced and how learning spaces need to be redefined and incorporated to support the tools of youth voice.

Careful selection of a tool that is of interest to teens creates an easy entry point for them to contribute to an activity in ways that connect with their lives and interests. For example, selecting Minecraft as a tool to teach principles of engineering, design, or architecture would likely result in a higher engagement from students in middle school due to the game's popularity with that age group. Young people who are interested in and have developed knowledge of Scratch benefit from the introduction of Hummingbird, a platform for learning robotics and engineering. This introduction helps to extend teen interest by linking programming with Scratch to physical objects such as robots.

As tools and ideas for learning are developed, it's important to consider the actual configuration of the room when fostering youth voice. A traditional classroom setting might not be the best configuration for a program aiming at creating a dynamic youth voice experience. Close attention needs to be given to configurations that provide:

- The opportunity to easily collaborate

- Ease of movement where the youth can decide where to engage in the activity

- Furniture that is modular and easy to move from place to place

- Easy access to the technology or tools for the program. Youth should feel free to use the tools and the adult should make them accessible.

## Youth Voice, Connected Learning, and Shared Purpose

The connected learning framework provides a foundation to create opportunities in which young people are learning based on their interests, but also in ways that adults working as facilitators of the learning can develop programs within the core principle of shared purpose and youth voice. Connected learning is also a framework that advocates for the use of digital media as a way to connect and build programs that encourage media creation, youth voice, and sharing. Connected learning

> advocates for broadened access to learning that is socially embedded, interest-driven, and oriented toward educational, economic, or political opportunity. Connected learning is realized when a young person is able to pursue a personal interest or passion with the support of friends and caring adults, and is in turn able to link this learning and interest to academic achievement, career success or civic engagement. This model is based on evidence that the most resilient, adaptive, and effective learning involves individual interest as well as social support to overcome adversity and provide recognition.[11]

In addition, connected learning "encourages cross-generational and cross-cultural groups to collaborate on projects and activities. A shared purpose can be demonstrated through collective goals, competitions, and cross-generational ownership."[12]

The current media landscape not only provides the opportunity to create cross-generational programs but also asks of providers to share learning outcomes. It also demands the implementation of a model in which the learning happens as collaboration. A media landscape is in constant change and requires letting go of the model of an expert in the room who holds all the knowledge about a subject, and instead moves to a model of shared learning experiences in which everyone contributes equally in the process of learning. On this topic, Ito et al. write:

> Social media and web-based communities provide unprecedented opportunities for cross-generational and cross-cultural learning and connection to unfold and thrive around common goals and interests:
>
> - Activities are organized around projects with a shared goal.
> - There are opportunities for students to create teams and compete, either at individual or group levels.
> - The learning experience supports cross-generational leadership and ownership.
> - Authority is distributed across student and adult spaces.[13]

It is important to note that in these last two points, the connected learning framework relates directly to the discussion in this chapter: the creation of programs with strong adult-youth partnerships to enhance youth voice.

With this shared purpose in mind, effective engagement is a collaboration, a shared desire to work together, to complete a project, to learn together. When discussing this shared purpose, Paulo Freire's statement in his *Pedagogy of the Oppressed* proves valuable. He writes, "Authentic education is not carried on by 'A' for 'B' or by 'A' about 'B,' but rather by 'A' *with* 'B' mediated by the world, a world that impresses and challenges both parties, giving rise to opinions about it."[14] We should strive to create a learning experience that it is democratic and equal, and in which the imparting of knowledge doesn't use a top-down model but is rather horizontal and democratic.

In my experience, the adage "you make the weather" might be one of the most useful tools for facilitating workshops with young people. When walking into a room to guide teens through a learning experience, the facilitator sets the tone on how students will take an interest in the program. I have been in workshops where the mood is so low that students lose enthusiasm. If the facilitator demonstrates engagement, excitement, and enthusiasm, it is likely the teens will follow. This engagement can only be achieved if the adult has an interest in the program and a shared purpose with the youth. The program serves the students and the adult facilitator equally. It is not only the adult who can shape the process and learning.

The interest-driven approach can only happen if young people have a voice and are able to clearly signal or articulate their interest. Dixie Ching and colleagues have described open-ended and direct ways in which youth signal their interests as well as their expertise and needs around that interest. On the subject of signaling, they write, "Youth are in many ways the main driver of support provision; support providers do not simply offer that support entirely on their own initiative—rather young people themselves play an active role."[15] The signals that teens send might range from what questions they ask, the kinds of tasks they volunteer to do, and what they produce for their digital artifact. The important point here is that young people are constantly communicating, broadcasting their youth voice, and that youth voice says a lot about their interests and engagement.

## Listening for Everything—Disengagement Equal to Engagement

Learning spaces, whether formal or informal, are places where youth-adult interactions produce levels of engagement that can lead to meaningful learning experiences. In order to create these meaningful experiences, the adult facilitator should practice a critical skill: listening. Of course, there's the listening for what students are saying when expressing their opinions. But a different kind of listening should also be practiced: listening for the non-verbal cues signaling teens' level of engagement and interest in what is happening in the workshop. When I spoke to Sara Vogel, she mentioned the notion of disengagement as a form of youth expression. "It is hard to think about it as a form of youth voice," Sara said, "but disengagement can tell you a lot about what the facilitator needs to change in a workshop, and to question why students are not connecting with the activity at hand." Furthermore, other factors have much to do with the sort of dynamic taking place during the learning. Every young person comes with a certain disposition to the learning. Knowing what those dispositions are will help maintain a program that encourages youth participation. The more teens feel heard, the more they will participate and be active learners. Hearing them requires being aware of other external factors in their lives. What is their situation at home? What is their cultural background? What is their relationship with learning spaces in general and to the particular space where your program is taking place?

Generally, when young people come to a program, providers tend to group them as the participants—the ones learning, the ones needing to develop skills. Differences are often not acknowledged or considered. Having a program in which each youth's personality, individuality, and background are considered when the program is delivered will build a youth-adult relationship that will be able to create products reflecting youth interests and their voice.

## Programs with Strong Youth-Adult Partnerships

The best way to achieve outcomes that incorporate a strong youth voice component are library programs that take place through a series of workshops where teens and adults come together for several sessions. Meaningful social bonds are more likely to develop if young people are engaged in a series taking place over longer periods of time. When this occurs, teens develop affinity with the adult facilitator(s) and with the institution as a whole. Creating an opportunity to connect in these ways provides youth with an implicit incentive to be part of the program and to fully engage, which will enable a richer and more productive experience. On the other hand, programs that take place one time only with a drop-in model make it difficult to develop lasting and meaningful youth-adult relationships.

Series programs do require more planning and more resources to be successful. Recruitment is critical: youth will be more likely to come and stay in the program if there are many other peers participating. The program also should be structured in ways that promotes socialization. It should feel different from school with room for teens to play and engage in a way that allows for conversations, includes interactive exercises, and provides opportunities to take control of learning.

## Figure 3-2. Icebreakers

### Mingle Mingle

1. While teens are mingling before the program starts, the facilitator calls a number from 1 to 4.

2. Teens then form groups made up of the number of people the facilitator has called.

3. The facilitator asks a question, and each group discusses the question.

4. After a minute of discussion, the facilitator selects some groups to talk about their discussion.

5. This should be repeated several times, changing the number called each time. As the number changes, teens have the chance to become a part of different groups and thereby meet and become connected to more of the participants.

### Human Barometer

1. On three pieces of paper write: AGREE, DISAGREE, NOT SURE.

2. Post the NOT SURE sign in the middle of a wall.

3. Post the AGREE and DISAGREE signs on the walls to the left and the right of the NOT SURE sign.

4. Ask teens what a barometer is.

5. Explain to the group that unlike a barometer that is used to measure air pressure, the Human Barometer will measure the pressure of opinion.

6. Read a statement and have teens move to the section that represents their opinion about it. Sample statements include: Teenagers only like playing video games that are violent; a game can express an idea just as well as a song, movie, or book; games can teach people about important issues; game designers have a responsibility for ideas expressed by their games.

7. Make sure the teens know the three rules of the activity:

   ○ When a teen picks a side, they should be prepared to explain why that side was selected.

- Teens can change sides if someone makes a compelling argument that changes their mind.

- The activity is not a debate but an opportunity to exchange opinions about various issues.

8. Go around the room asking a few teens from each side to explain why they agree, disagree, or are not sure.

9. Repeat a few times, having teens continue to move around the room.

## Smack the Mosquito

The purpose of this game is to work together as a team, test reflexes and attention, and keep a rhythm going.

1. Get everyone into a circle.

2. Have the teens imagine that there is a mosquito over someone's head.

3. The person with the mosquito over their head has to duck to avoid the mosquito while the two people next to him/her have to clap their hands together to "smack" the mosquito.

4. Then the mosquito moves to the next person's head and the same thing repeats until everyone in the circle has gone.

5. Keep playing until there is a good rhythm going.

Other elements to consider for the success of the program include the following:

- Clear objectives defined as outcomes for the program (see chapter 5 for more on this topic)

- Agile curriculum that is easily adaptable for a variety of situations and young people

- Engagement efforts across the community that leads to high attendance and retention

- Facilitator comfort, excitement, and familiarity with program

- A program design that harnesses connected learning approaches

- Intrinsic motivational approaches so teens want to join and stay in the program

One technique to cultivate learning environments that support strong youth-to-youth and youth-to-adult relationships is to include socialization time at the beginning of workshops. A key to this it to NOT start content delivery until after this initial time purposefully spent on meeting and hanging out. This can help teens feel more welcome. (See figure 3-2 for icebreaker examples.)

Allowing young people to form relationships with their peers should be a priority in program design and a key factor in developing youth voice. The adult facilitator should plan and/or be aware of the need to create an atmosphere in which teens are able to talk to each other, know each other on a personal level, and learn about their common interests. Icebreakers encourage social interactions, create team-building opportunities, provide the chance to collaborate and solve problems, and are good for group discussions.

## Equity and Adult Intervention in Youth Voice

Consider the case of a young woman interviewing for a new position. She just finished college and is excited and eager to start working. She does well on the interview, is called back, and offered a job. The salary is revealed to her. There's room to offer more, but only if she requests it. When the salary is presented to her, she accepts it right away without negotiating. What's the reason? Too much eagerness to have her first job? The need to start a job right away? Whatever the case, would previous exposure to express her own ideas, to voice her needs, and to talk things through help the young woman negotiate a better salary? Could youth voice promote the type of confidence and assertiveness needed in this situation? Would previous opportunities to build her voice have given this woman the chance to pursue a better outcome? Opportunities for young people to become citizens prepared to enter the workforce with a strong voice could potentially have an effect on larger personal and professional socioeconomic outcomes. I would argue that young people who are accustomed to articulating and sharing their ideas are more likely to successfully and effectively make their needs heard by others, especially adults. This can be accomplished by creating spaces in which youth-adult partnerships encourage young people to express themselves freely, to identify their needs, and clearly determine when it is important and necessary to voice their ideas or concerns.

## Progressively Creating Trust

In order to maintain youth interest in programs, library staff working with teens must form strong and meaningful partnerships. Adults belong to a different domain than young people, and they share certain dispositions, social norms, and values. Domains in this case are the set of values, cultural norms, and social constructs that form part of the behaviors of both young people and adults participating in the learning. As programs take place over time in a series of workshops, adults and teens will begin to share their domain progressively. For example, the fact that an adult is an avid video game player and that there's a youth in the program playing the same games can create a connection, an immediate identification of interests. This commonality over video games can inform the learning and make strong connections between the youth and adult provider. It can inform the learning while developing stronger bonds. However, it should be kept within the limits of the learning experience and not cross to a more personal relationship that is no longer rooted in the learning experience.

Over time, through social interactions, team building, and shared interests, the domains begin to merge. Since adults' and young people's social domains are different, they do not converge fully, but it must be the goal of the learning experience to share as much of each other's social domain as possible while maintaining social boundaries that create a strong and trusting relationship.

As the program continues, teens and adults can begin to closely share their domains. Learning together, collaborating, and creating new social relationships would help move adult and youth domains closer as the partnerships become stronger.

However, because adults and teens are in different domains, we must ask whether they can share them at 100%. It might be more realistic to consider that the majority of their domain would be shared but certain parts would remain separate. This is not only practical but also necessary to maintaining social boundaries for the success of a program that doesn't blur the nature of the youth-adult relationship.

## Figure 3-3. Building Relationships and Merging Adult-Youth Domains

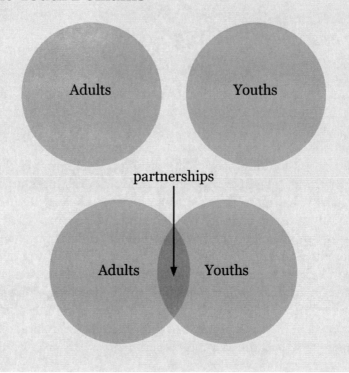

## Figure 3-4. Building Relationships: Merged Adult-Youth Domains

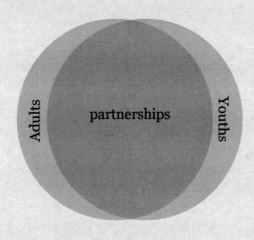

# Youth Voice as a Collective Experience

## Global Kids Youth Conference

Every year the nonprofit organization Global Kids in New York City holds a youth conference, and each year the conference has a social issue theme such as immigration, global warming, war, and so on. The conference consists of a series of workshops led and planned by youth who participate in after-school and in-school programs. For months prior to the conference, adult facilitators and youth leaders conduct workshops to plan the conference. During those workshops, students brainstorm the theme of the conference, plan workshops, and practice opening remarks, which are usually in the form of a skit. They also plan and design the event for the day, which includes plenaries with performances and speeches by young people and adults.

The day of the conference, there are workshops led by students with guest speakers who take part in a discussion around the theme of the conference. The conference is attended by an average of 500 students from schools in New York City. It is a day full of activity, with teens getting excited about the performances. It has the feeling of a celebration, and students from different parts of New York come together to mingle and learn about the conference theme. It is an event full of energy and fun. Adults who support the youth participants during the conference understand that the conference is completely run by teens. There's an unspoken rule that adults must observe as the workshop develops. Sometimes when the workshop runs into problems, the adults let the teens figure it out, and sometimes they fail.

During one of these workshops, I saw a coworker step in and help the students. Another coworker turned to me and said, "I think that's cheating." Is it really cheating? Would the teens learn more by failing or if they have a successful workshop? Would they feel inclined to conduct a similar workshop if they figure it out on their own or if they get the help they need from an adult to complete the workshop successfully? It depends on the experience and disposition of the teens. Here is when the adult should become a good listener, aware of the needs of the young people. Identify if they have the tools to adjust the workshop, handle behavioral issues with their peers, deliver the content with confidence, remember the content, and move through the content in a way that their audience has a clear road map to the learning objectives set at the

# Figure 3-5. Case 2: The Case of the Evil Agents—Identifying Moments in Which Youth Feel Heard

I was leading a series of workshops with a group of middle school students at the High Point branch of the Seattle Public library to design a location-based game using the platform TaleBlazer. Groups were assigned the task of creating characters for a story. They were designing a game to take place at a small park a few blocks from the library. The theme of the game had been decided: community helping the environment. Working in groups, the students wrote their core ideas about the game. The story centered on a storm that destroyed the environment in their neighborhood. Environmentally friendly features, such as swales, were part of the park redesign that took place when the neighborhood was rebuilt in the early 2000s. The player had to collect items to fix environmental problems still plaguing the park. These items were given by community members that players encountered throughout the park during game play. I worked with a co-facilitator to synthesize the ideas presented by the young people. We took that synthesis and turned it into a cohesive single-game core idea. Game mechanics were also decided: the player would walk around the park with the goal of fixing environmental problems such as rescuing a fallen tree or unclogging a storm drain. In order to fix the problems, the player had to collect tools (a rope, a rake, etc.) from community members who wanted to maintain the park in good condition. The game was over when all the problems in the park were fixed, similar to cleaning the park of problems. A paper prototype with these features was also created.

After presenting the teens with the concept for the game, getting their feedback, and hearing that they liked it, we asked them to work on fleshing out the story and creating characters. When it was time to share the work with all, one of the groups presented evil agents. My immediate reaction was one of shock and confusion. Where did they come from? These evil agents were not part of the activity. What did they have to do with the game? Nothing, I told myself. Now, how are we going to tell the kids that the work they had done was not going to be part of the game. But then, when ending the workshop, I told them we had a new game design challenge: What should we do with the evil agents?

I continued to work with the co-facilitator on the project, which entailed taking the ideas the teens had provided, giving them shape, organizing them, and creating a paper prototype of the game. When it came time to discuss the evil agents, we decided they definitely needed to be part of the final game. But what should we do with them? So, we brainstormed. What if the evil agents prevented the player from fixing the environmental problems? What if they stole the tools that the community helpers gave out? We decided it was the right solution: The evil agents would appear at random places in the park. When a player got close to an evil agent, the agent would appear and take the tool the player had collected.

Including the evil agents not only made the game more fun and engaging; it also turned it into a game made and created by teens. Showing them how the evil agents were incorporated into the game was thrilling to the students. Allowing their ideas and content to make it into the game gave them ownership and also agency. They were the producers of media, of a location-based game with elements decided and created by them. We as adult facilitators helped them along the way.

It was a great lesson for me as a designer and facilitator of learning: Had we not allowed the freedom for the students to work on their own characters, they would not have come up with the evil agents and the game would not have been as good as it is. Facilitating this type of learning is a delicate process: There are times in which youth need structure; with vague instructions, they can feel lost and become easily frustrated and discouraged, which can lead to disengagement. There are other times when giving teens few instructions is a good thing. In these instances, asking youth to come up with their own ideas leads to the emergence of new and fresh concepts, concepts from their own perspective, based on their own interests and experience. It is the role of the adult facilitator to identify the level of structure required to help the youth designers along the way and, at the same time, allow for spontaneity and creativity to flourish.

Including evil agents in the game was a departure from the original concept of the game. When giving liberty to the youth participants, they came up with a new element, surprising and unexpected. From a facilitator point of view, the first reaction was to dismiss their input. Incorporating the evil agents meant that the original concept had to be modified. Given the time frame to release the game, incorporating the evil agents in the game posed a challenge. It might be easier to not include them in the game. However, not incorporating them would have been detrimental to both the end product and for embedding youth voice in the program.

start. Based on those assessments, the adult can make the decision to assist the youth facilitators or let them solve the problem on their own.

Although the conference provides great opportunities as a platform for teens to express themselves and feel they have accomplished something of relevance, it is perhaps important for the adults to give more support during the workshops without overtaking the leadership role from the students running the event.

## Emoti-Con

Emoti-Con is a digital media and technology showcase event that takes place every year in New York City. "Each year, over 150 New York City youth from programs throughout the five boroughs compete in the premier showcase of digital media and technology projects designed by youth, for the betterment of the world."[16]

At Emoti-Con, young people have the opportunity to present projects created mostly in after-school programs around New York City to a diverse and large audience. The conference is visited by educators, practitioners, and other students. As part of the planning for the event, teens from different organizations in New York City come together to plan and organize it. The teens are also emcees for the day, and they design activities to warm up the audience at the start of the conference.

What makes Emoti-Con a unique opportunity to strengthen youth voice is the fact that the event is designed to include several entry points for young people who want to be involved. They can choose to be leaders and be part of the planning committee. They can present their projects to their peers and explain their concepts to adult judges. They can be selected as finalists and deliver a pitch to explain their project to the general audience.

The day of the festival, youth participants set up their projects to be viewed by festival attendees, some of them jurors. The jury selects the best projects, and the teens go to the stage and pitch the project. The jurors provide feedback, and there's a ballot for all the young people attending the festival to select winning projects in several categories: crowd favorite, point of view, most entertaining, most innovative, and best pitch.

## Figure 3-6. Case 3: Ice Cream and Ketchup

I was leading a program at the Magnolia branch of the Seattle Public Library where teens were deciding on a story for the game they were creating. They had previously been given parameters for what they would create: the game should take place in a certain location, must be about that location, should have a message, and should give the player interesting choices. Interesting choices in games give players agency, providing opportunity to change the outcome of the game. The choices should feel seamless and integrated into the game story and the overall game experience. After much debate and brainstorming, the teens decided that the game would include memes and that it would involve a time machine and an evil scientist. However, they weren't sure what message a player would get from playing the game. For that reason we reintroduced the concept of theme in works of art, including novels like *Harry Potter* and comics like *Spider-Man*. It was hard to "reverse engineer" the game to include a message, but the majority of the teens' ideas were included in the final project. The program lasted eight weeks, which is a short time to produce a complex game. Still the game was finished and the youth participants were very excited about seeing their idea come to fruition. At some point during the development, one of them wanted to introduce a tsunami event and a Donald Trump character. I asked the group if they believed that those elements fit the game concept. Much debate took place, and I came up with an example to help them understand the concept of a cohesive story line. "If you are using a recipe," I said, "would you add an ingredient that would not go with the dish? What if, for example, you added ketchup to macaroni and cheese?" "I would totally add ketchup to my macaroni and cheese," answered the youth advocating for the tsunami and Donald Trump character. "But what about ketchup on ice cream?" a girl asked. "Exactly," I told them. "Would you add ketchup to ice cream?" I used the analogy to control their impulses to go off topic. Every time they wanted to add something departing from the main concept of the game and introduce a new idea, I would ask them if it was a "ketchup on ice cream" idea. They would pause and think carefully about the content and how it fit the overall concept of the game. It was a necessary intervention—one getting at the core of how to structure a game with elements connecting to form a cohesive experience for the player.

Educators must not impose their ideas on students, but they have the role of guiding them and helping them understand certain techniques and practices as part of their craft. Video games, films, essays, short stories—they all have an inner structure, and educators can provide the guidance that young people need as they begin to learn about the production of media texts.

There are certain programmatic realities to be considered when delivering a program. A program is planned to last a certain number of weeks, and a capstone event is part of the planning, a common youth development practice. Project-based programs such as game design require a complete product to present during the capstone event. There are times when incorporating youth voice fully might derail the project, and the facilitator has to become the leader to make sure timelines are met to have a complete product at the end of the program. Teens might not be aware of the external circumstances that the program must meet in order to be completed. At libraries, it is particularly important to keep the schedule on track since library staff are often scheduled to take different roles and are assigned to those roles in advance. There are few opportunities to extend or modified the schedule in the program. Such factors can play a role on how to navigate youth voice as the program is delivered.

Events such as Emoti-Con provide a platform for youth voice to be expressed as part of a community. Youth come together and begin to form an identity around the use of digital media to express their ideas, to articulate those ideas to their peers and judges, and to enter in a competition. Creating such events at libraries would help build interest in the programs offered and would provide those working on a project an intrinsic incentive to participate in programs offered at the library.

## Community Voice as Part of Library Offerings

When implementing programs that incorporate youth voice, library staff are in a unique position to design programs that connect with youth interest while at the same time addressing community needs.

With access to diverse populations—a community of parents, caregivers, young adults, immigrant families, and non-dominant youth—the library can become a hub for the delivery of programs rich in content, providing learning experiences related to young people's everyday life, incorporating their voices, and meeting the needs of the community served.

Just like the youth-adult partnerships previously discussed, community-library partnerships should be informed by a highly collaborative framework. For example, if a library hosts a community listening event, it cannot be a one-way conversation. It is important to identify the needs of the community, the interests and needs of youth, and where there are gaps that the library can help to fill. Programs designed with clear outcomes can move this conversation forward and as a result align community and youth needs and interests with the mission and vision of the library. Because youth voice connects teens who are a part of a community together with a library program, these activities at their core support community needs by designing programs with a strong youth voice.

In addition, if programs are aligned with high-level goals that connect community, youth, and the library, it is likely that staff working with teens will be able to secure stronger institutional support. Being able to show that through youth voice the library is having an impact on the entire community helps to demonstrate overall value. Having institutional support makes the implementation of the program easier for library staff and more relevant and successful to the community and the youth served.

## Conclusion

A set of values from home, school, and community play a role in the way young people engage and participate during learning programs. Acknowledging and taking into consideration these values helps in creating an environment in which youth feel supported and heard. Therefore, they will be more willing to express their ideas. Once they are able to express their ideas and connect to the content in personal ways, teens will not only actively participate in a program—they will continue building on their interests and forging pathways as they seek to strengthen their academic, career, and life goals.

Youth voice can take many forms and be incorporated in learning experiences at various degrees. At the core of youth voice is the relationship that the adult facilitator forms with young people who enter the social space of learning environments. In order to achieve these partnerships, many strategies can be incorporated into the practice of a facilitator working with youth participants. Critical strategies include the intentional creation of social relationships with students: relationships built over time will produce a program where young people trust the adult and are conducive to a dynamic leading to better learning outcomes. When the young person trusts the adult, a richer exchange of ideas can occur, which can then lead to a program resulting in a stronger youth point of view. In addition to youth-adult relationships, adults can also acknowledge and be aware of the different socioeconomic, social, and cultural norms that adults and teens bring to the learning space. Having this awareness helps create spaces where the program enhances those aspects rather than ignores them. When these factors are intentionally taken into consideration, learning spaces change from a model with the adult as an expert who delivers knowledge from top to bottom, to one in which the learning happens in a collaborative space and the learning becomes a collective experience. This in turn can help create a place where persistent models of social inequalities begin to be addressed and eliminated. Only when we move away from the traditional model of adult as expert, or adult as decision maker, can we begin to create programs built on the cultural and social needs of young people participating in the learning experiences that enhance youth voice.

## Notes

1. Paulo Freire, *Pedagogy of the Oppressed*, chap. 3, http://www.historyisaweapon.com/defcon2/pedagogy/pedagogychapter3.html (accessed February 22, 2017).

2. National Center for Education Statistics, "Fast Facts: Back to School Statistics," https://nces.ed.gov/fastfacts/display.asp?id=372 (accessed February 22, 2017).

3. Afterschool Alliance, *America after 3 PM: Afterschool Programs in Demand* (2014), http://www.afterschoolalliance.org/documents/aa3pm-2014/aa3pm_national_report.pdf (accessed February 22, 2017).

4. Peter A. Witt and Linda L. Caldwell, *Recreation and Youth Development* (State College, PA: Venture, 2005).

5. Sara Vogel, interview by author, fall 2016.

6. Rachel Bolstad, "From 'Student Voice' to 'Youth-Adult Partnership,'" *Set* 1 (2011): 31–33, http://www.nzcer.org.nz/system/files/set2011_1_031.pdf (accessed February 22, 2017).

7. Ibid.

8. Dana L. Mitra, "Collaborating with Students: Building Youth-Adult Partnerships in Schools," *American Journal of Education* 115, no. 3 (2009): 407–36, doi:10.1086/597488.

9. Bolstad, "From 'Student Voice' to 'Youth-Adult Partnership'"; text modified to apply to informal learning spaces such as libraries and museums.

10. Mizuko Ito, Kris Gutiérrez, Sonia Livingstone, Bill Penuel, Jean Rhodes, Katie Salen, Juliet Schor, Julian Sefton-Green, and S. Craig Watkins, *Connected Learning: An Agenda for Research and Design* (Digital Media and Learning Research Hub, January 2013), http://dmlhub.net/wp-content/uploads/files/Connected_Learning_report.pdf (accessed February 22, 2017).

11. Ibid.

12. Kiley Larson, Mizuko Ito, Eric Brown, Mike Hawkins, Nichole Pinkard, and Penny Sebring, *Safe Space and Shared Interests: YOUmedia Chicago as a Laboratory for Connected Learning* (Digital Media and Learning Research Hub, 2013), https://dmlhub.net/wp-content/uploads/files/SAFE-SPACE-final-with-addenda.pdf (accessed April 13, 2017).

13. Mizuko Ito, Kiley Larson, Eric Brown, Mike Hawkins, Nicole Pinkard, and Penny Sebring, *Safe Space and Shared Interests: YOUmedia Chicago as a Laboratory for Connected Learning* (Digital Media and Learning Research Hub, November 2013), http://dmlhub.net/wp-content/uploads/files/SAFE-SPACE-final-with-addenda.pdf (accessed February 22, 2017).

14. Freire, *Pedagogy of the Oppressed*.

15. Dixie Ching, Kylie Pepper, and Chris Hoadly, "'He Saw I Had a Loving for It': Youth Signaling as a Means of Generating Social Support around Interest-Driven Learning Pathways with Technology," forthcoming, *Hive Research Lab*, https://hiveresearchlab.org/.

16. Emoti-Con, http://emoti-con.org/ (accessed February 22, 2017).

SAN DIEGO (CA) PUBLIC LIBRARY

# IDEA Lab Tech Team Internship

MONNEE TONG

## What Did You Want to Achieve?

The goal of the IDEA Lab Tech Team Internship is to teach new technology skills to teens and help them to cement those skills by having the opportunity to teach their peers. As the program progresses, our hope is to connect the interns to the greater professional community to help them realize their interests can turn into career opportunities.

## Overview of the Program/Project

The IDEA Lab Tech Team Internship is a teen internship program at San Diego Central Library. It was developed for e3 Civic High students, the charter school that is housed in the same building as the library. Teens who are a part of the IDEA Lab Tech Team develop twenty-first-century skills by receiving training from community partner Media Arts Center San Diego. As a result of this training and opportunity to create content, since 2014 the teens have created

- four videos;

- fifteen workshops for peers (including introductory workshops on iMovie, GarageBand, and Photoshop, as well as on how to use a drawing tablet);

- the exhibit *Citizens of Central*, a spin-off of *Humans of New York*, that focuses on Central Library staff;

- a coloring book with scenes from downtown San Diego.

## What Challenges Did You Face and How Did You Overcome Them?

Absenteeism and keeping teens on track to complete their projects have been challenging. Our first year was the most challenging, because the expectations weren't clear enough for the teens. After that first year, I had a meeting with each intern and outlined the expectations we had for them. We had the teens sign contracts that stated they were committed to completing the program.

## What Did You Learn?

So much! We learned that over time the interns slowly took ownership of the IDEA Lab and wanted to see it succeed. We also learned that the teens found the soft skills they learned from the internship just as valuable as the technology skills they acquired. When asked what they remember most about being an intern, many of them commented on some aspect of teamwork or collaboration.

## How Does This Work Connect to YALSA's Futures Report and Vision?

We are inspired by connected learning, which is outlined in *The Future of Library Services for and with Teens: A Call to Action.* We use connected learning as a guide to how we approach teen services. In that type of library, staff become active participants in teen learning by being connectors, mentors, and cheerleaders.

The IDEA Lab Tech Team Internship is an example of how we've incorporated connected learning. The program provides a safe space for self-directed, interest-driven learning for students who may not have had the chance to explore new skills or future career options without it. We've moved beyond being a place to simply check out books by providing a place where teens can create, be engaged, discover and learn, or simply hang out. It's essential that librarians are there for teens, not only to assist them with their information needs, but to be their guides in making the connection between what sparks their interests and future careers.

> "The IDEA Lab prepared me for the real world because I have to work with other people to get a project done."

> "We've moved beyond being a place to simply check books out by providing a place where teens can create, be engaged, discover and learn, or simply hang out."

# CHAPTER 4
# Engaging with Community

JESSI SNOW, WITH CONTRIBUTIONS BY
SHANNON PETERSON

## Introduction

YALSA's report *The Future of Library Services for and with Teens: A Call to Action*[1] (referred to as the *Futures Report*) calls for libraries to take bold action in order to help teens build the skills and knowledge they'll need in school, careers, and life. These actions include bridging the growing knowledge divide, building on teens' motivation to learn, providing workforce development training, and serving as the connector between teens and other community agencies; they may also require significant changes to the types of programs and services being offered as well as the process by which they are identified, planned, and evaluated. This can feel a bit daunting, especially considering the reality of limited staff capacity that many public and school libraries face. The good news is that this is work that's most successfully undertaken within the context of community and with the support, input, guidance, and expertise of teens, parents, colleagues, community stakeholders, and more. In *Community Solutions for Opportunity Youth*, a report written by the White House Council for Community Solutions, council member Paul Schmitz argues: "We have to recognize that to transform young people's lives, it's not individual programs or individual interventions; it's community and supportive relationships."[2]

For many libraries, adapting to a focus on community relationships requires a fundamental shift in philosophy. Rather than providing services to a community, the emphasis becomes working toward shared goals *with* the community. Doing this is not a one-and-done scenario; it requires time, flexibility, open-mindedness, skill development, and an eye toward long-term strategy and ongoing collaboration.

This chapter focuses on why community engagement is an essential component of the work that libraries need to do for and with teens. It begins with a call to action for the important work that lies ahead and provides context to support that work. If you're:

- shifting gears from your regular way of doing things,

- need to advocate getting away from the desk,

- working to demonstrate specific teen needs to a potential funder,

you'll have the information you need to advocate successfully with colleagues, administrators, decision makers, and funders.

Next, the chapter focuses on the nuts and bolts of how to get started with community engagement. From testing assumptions about your community through data collection and asset mapping, to fostering participation by parents, young people, and stakeholders, these activities should become the core of how you adapt, learn, and evolve community engagement work over time. Remember that this is not a prescription for success. Just as every community is different, so, too, will be the way you navigate the engagement process. This chapter provides a framework for that, no matter who you are working with and what your goals are for that work.

## Defining Community Engagement

Before going any further, it's important to ensure that it's clear what "engagement" means within the context of community engagement. It's true that libraries have always been invested in free and open access as well as meaningful outreach to their communities. After all, pioneering teen librarian Margaret Edwards drove a horse-drawn wagon through the streets of Baltimore to reach teens with barriers of access to the library's physical location. Library outreach and marketing are important and can certainly have a place in future-focused library service, but it's important to recognize the difference between engagement and outreach.

Shifting from the idea of the library as an institution that "informs" others to an institution that "empowers" others will not happen overnight. The "Community Engagement Assessment Tool," developed as a part of the Building the Field of community engagement partners project, is a useful resource for determining where an organization fits on the outreach to community engagement spectrum. The tool highlights categories of engagement and asks those assessing their engagement strategies to consider the following:

- The kind of relationships they have with community members—with an eye toward considering if those relationships are transactional or foundational, not inclusive or diverse, and short term or long term.

- Why people are being engaged: to reach a specific goal or to create space for people to connect, raise questions, build power, and act in their own interests.

- How and when people are getting involved: thinking about whether or not those involvement opportunities are more passive (e.g., surveys and flyers) or more active (e.g., listening sessions). This section of the tool also asks users to consider if involvement by the community starts after something has been planned or actually is a part of the planning process.

- How ideas are generated: Are the ideas about working with community on a project generated solely by staff, or do staff empower community members to come up with ideas and reflect on what is happening in the community?

- How organizational policies have an impact on community engagement work: with the outreach end of the spectrum demonstrating a less flexible approach to policies and the community engagement end of the spectrum focused on an approach that is flexible and responsive.[3]

In true community engagement, community members are not simply informed about the work the library does; they are involved in designing and implementing that work. A quality community engagement builds upon the capacity, expertise, and insight of the entire community. The focus then is not on the library as provider but on the community agreeing on common goals for programs and services that support the needs of young people across the community.

Take, for example, the following scenarios about Smallville, USA—a community with a robust agricultural economy and that is now seeing an influx of Spanish-speaking migrant workers:

*Scenario A:* Smallville Library is aware of the growth of the migrant worker population and sets aside resources to increase the number of dollars spent on Spanish-language materials. The Smallville Library also hires a staff member to host monthly Spanish-language story times at the library. Along with these, library staff attend outreach events at schools and local churches targeted to the Spanish-speaking population. At these events, library staff talk up services to encourage library usage. Despite all of this, Spanish-language materials sit on the shelves and the turnout for Spanish-language story time is low. In fact, the few attendees of this story time tend to be English-speaking children looking to learn a second language. Library staff therefore decide there is just not enough interest from this community in what they have to offer and slowly phase out the increased attention on Spanish-language materials and programs.

*Scenario B:* Smallville Library is aware of the growth of the migrant worker population and over time develops relationships with stakeholders in the community specifically working with that population. Library staff build these relationships by intentionally setting aside time to communicate with other organizations and community members. Staff also attend outside events and meetings on a regular basis—for example, meetings of out-of-school-time organizations that host programs for the children of migrant workers. These relationships enable the library to connect with community members and host "listening sessions" to hear what community members think is most important when it comes to the needs of teens. Following these sessions, the library is able to work with other organizations and community members to design services that meet the needs expressed in the sessions and build on the assets of all those involved. Community organizations and members agree to goals for teen services across the community.

**Figure 4-1. The Spectrum of Community Engagement**
Increasing Impact on Decision Making

| Informing | Consulting | Involving | Collaborating | Empowering |
|---|---|---|---|---|
| Providing balanced and objective information about new programs or services and about the reasons for choosing them. Providing updates during implementation. | Inviting feedback on alternatives, analyses, and decisions related to new programs or services. Letting people know how their feedback has influenced program decisions. | Working with community members to ensure that their aspirations and concerns are considered at every stage of planning and decision making. Letting people know how their involvement has influenced program decisions. | Enabling community members to participate in every aspect of planning and decision making for new programs or services. | Giving community members decision-making authority on new programs or services and allowing professionals to serve in consultative or supportive roles. |

*Source:* https://ssir.org/articles/entry/community_engagement_matters_now_more_than_ever

Needless to say, Scenario A demonstrates traditional marketing and outreach of library planned activities. While the library is tapped into changing demographics and has valuable insight and expertise to support probable needs, there is a lack of relationship with and trust from the community that they need to reach. In Scenario B, the library is truly occupied in active engagement with the community. The process of getting to a solution and a set of services takes longer than what occurs in Scenario A. However, the time spent pays off in a sustainable set of services that are offered across the community and serve actual stated teen needs.

It's important to note that community engagement is not one specific set of actions. It is a process by which community members are given increasing opportunities to engage in decision making. The chart below from the *Stanford Social Innovation Review* outlines a continuum for moving from outreach to community engagement.

# Taking the Community Engagement Leadership Role

Being a community engagement leader in your library and community may be a challenge. However, one way to help bring others along is to focus on the needs of teens and why it takes an entire community together to support those needs.

In order to discuss teen needs with community members and colleagues, it's important to be aware of trends related to the lives of adolescents. As you begin to develop relationships, design new initiatives, and track your efforts, keeping up with trends will help you to identify challenges and opportunities, and will provide the language for why you may need to rethink existing efforts. Below are some examples of national trends to get started with.

## Diversity

The 2014 U.S. Census reported that those ages five years old and under became the United States' first minority-majority for the first time, with 50.2% being part of a minority race or ethnic group.[4] Further, children and youth living in immigrant families are the fastest growing group of American children.[5]

## Equity

In 2015, 5,527,000, or one in seven, teens and young adults in the United States were classified as disconnected or "opportunity" youth, those ages 16–24 who are not in school and not working. Costs associated with opportunity youth (incarceration, Medicaid, public assistance payments, and Supplemental Security Income payments) were estimated to cost taxpayers $26.8 billion in 2013 alone.[6] Given the disproportionality of students of color facing school disciplinary issues,[7] struggling with poverty,[8] and residing within the juvenile justice system,[9] it should hardly come as a surprise that youth disconnection rates for blacks (21.6%), Native Americans (27.8%), and Latinos (16.3%) are markedly higher than rates for Asian Americans (7.9%) or whites (11.3%).[10] As the minority-majority population of youth of color grows into adolescence within systems that support disconnection, the number of opportunity youth is therefore at serious risk of increasing.

## Culture and Careers

The evolution of industry and innovation in the 21st century has fundamentally shifted how we work in addition to the knowledge and skills that are required. In the United States, 11.5 million of the 11.6 million jobs created since the Great Recession have required at least some post-secondary education.[11] Further, STEM-related jobs are expected to vastly outpace non-STEM-related growth, with an estimated 9 million new jobs by 2022.[12] Yet in a study of high school students done in the 2010–11 and 2014–15 school years, less than half of participants felt prepared for college and careers.[13]

Technology has also had a major impact on how youth access information, socialize, and create identity. Lacking physical spaces and opportunities, young people rely on social media in order to connect, communicate, and build community. According to the "Common Sense Census: Media Use by Teens" survey from Common Sense Media, American teens use an average of nine hours of media per day, not including for school or homework.[14]

Helping all teens—especially those with the most barriers to building skills, forming positive relationships, and increasing self-efficacy—is work that libraries absolutely can and must take on, and working with the community is an essential part of that. If there is one thing to remember in this entire chapter, it's this:

> Teen library workers are inherently awesome, but there is no one magical human who can untangle large societal issues and design programs and services with impact that achieve deep and lasting outcomes. It's not possible to do it alone.

Let that really sink in. Is it a relief to realize that you don't need to help teens succeed in life all by yourself? As a library staff member serving teens, instead of trying to do everything on your own, think about how you can best learn to understand the needs of teens, communicate those needs to others, and enlist a broad spectrum of engaged people in the community to help you problem solve, adapt, and transform local efforts over time. Instead of being the expert in all things teen, become an agent of change within the full community. Engage a team of adults and teens together. Programs and services won't depend solely on you, but will build from the strength of the relationships you've developed. Develop what Howard Fuller, a former superintendent of Milwaukee Public Schools and a prominent school reform leader, would call a sense of "patient urgency." He states:

> If you aren't patient, you only get illusory change. Lasting change is not possible without community. You may be gone in 5 or 10 years, but the community will still be there. You need a sense of urgency to push the process forward and maintain momentum.[15]

## Getting Started with Community Engagement

Now that you have a basic understanding of what community engagement is (and isn't), and an understanding of why it's important, it's time to start thinking about how to actually get started. It's important to recognize from the beginning and to communicate to your supervisors and team that it's unlikely this process will be linear or that any of this work will be the kind that you can check off of a to-do list and call it done. That's not to say that there won't be milestones to celebrate or important achievements met, but true community engagement implies that you'll be working through issues that impact a community. Those issues may morph, evolve, or secede, but there will always be issues. This will mark the beginning of working through that change together, rather than reacting to it from one position or organization. Taking the time to understand, plan, and reflect through each of the elements below will help you to move forward in a sustainable way.

## Build Cultural Competence

Community engagement cannot happen without cultural competence or a clear understanding of the impact that race and culture have had on you and others, as well as an ability to develop meaningful relationships with diverse populations. As bell hooks notes, "To build community requires vigilant awareness of the work we must continually do to undermine all the socialization that leads us to behave in ways that perpetuate domination."[16]

If you're reading this, it's likely that you are white and probably female. According to data provided by the American Library Association in its 2012 "Diversity Counts" analysis, the field of librarianship continues to be an overwhelmingly homogeneous one, with 88% of credentialed librarians working in the nation's public, academic, and school libraries identifying as non-Hispanic white in 2009 (a decrease of 1% from 2000).[17] Although some may argue that this homogeneity is reflected in higher education in general, MLIS attainment trends actually lie in opposition to overall master's level education, which showed a decrease from 77% attainment by whites in 2002–3 to 69% in 2012–13 and a dramatic increase by Hispanic and African American students during the same period.[18]

As the youth population moves toward majority-minority, this stubborn lack of diversity in the field becomes even more of a concern. Despite the best of intentions (and of course we have them—we are librarians, after all), it can be a challenge to recognize the perks and advantages afforded to whites in our society and the invisible disadvantages or barriers that people of color may be facing. In *White Anti-Racist Activism: A Personal Roadmap*, author Jennifer R. Holladay describes white privilege this way:

> White skin privilege is not something that white people necessarily do, create or enjoy on purpose. Unlike the more overt individual and institutional manifestations of racism . . . , white skin privilege is a transparent preference for whiteness that saturates our society. White skin privilege serves several functions. First, it provides white people with "perks" that we do not earn and that people of color do not enjoy. Second, it creates real advantages for us. White people are immune to a lot of challenges. Finally,

white privilege shapes the world in which we live—the way that we navigate and interact with one another and with the world.[19]

In her foundational work on the subject, *White Privilege: Unpacking the Invisible Knapsack*,[20] Peggy McIntosh describes examples of the "perks and advantages" that were not necessarily afforded to her African American friends and colleagues, friends, and acquaintances:

1. I can if I wish arrange to be in the company of people of my race most of the time.

2. If I should need to move, I can be pretty sure of renting or purchasing housing in an area which I can afford and in which I would want to live.

3. I can be pretty sure that my neighbors in such a location will be neutral or pleasant to me.

4. I can go shopping alone most of the time, pretty well assured that I will not be followed or harassed.

5. I can turn on the television or open to the front page of the paper and see people of my race widely represented.

6. When I am told about our national heritage or about "civilization," I am shown that people of my color made it what it is.

7. I can go into a music shop and count on finding the music of my race represented, into a supermarket and find the staple foods that fit with my cultural traditions, into a hairdresser's shop and find someone who can cut my hair.

8. I can arrange to protect my children most of the time from people who might not like them.

9. I can swear, or dress in second-hand clothes, or not answer letters, without having people attribute these choices to the bad morals, the poverty, or the illiteracy of my race.

10. I can do well in a challenging situation without being called a credit to my race.

11. I am never asked to speak for all the people of my racial group.

12. I can be pretty sure that if I ask to talk to "the person in charge," I will be facing a person of my race.

13. If a traffic cop pulls me over or if the IRS audits my tax return, I can be sure I haven't been singled out because of my race.

As evidenced in the breadth of these examples, privilege is deeply ingrained and pervasive in our society. As you reflect and build an awareness of the impact of privilege on your own experience, begin to think through the implicit biases that you may carry as a result. The human brain, with its desire to categorize, can reinforce unconscious attitudes about people or groups who are different or outside one's own sociocultural sphere. These attitudes then lead to the patterns of inequity or unintentional support of structural racism. Taking time to deeply self-assess and to build a personal learning or advocating for an organizational training plan related to social justice will be an essential step in being able to effectively build relationships with and integrate the experience of your full community.

As you take stock of the role of culture in your own life, you can also think about ways to develop or deepen relationships with community members from other cultures. For example, you might do the following:

- *Reroute regular habits:* Find stores, restaurants, or events where you might experience and come into contact with people from outside your regular network. This may also help you empathize with the experience of being a minority.

- *Ask questions and listen:* Everyone appreciates someone taking a genuine interest in their perspective, preferences, and story.

- *Be sensitive to different communication styles:* Think about how you might approach conversations or meetings in such a way that helps everyone feel comfortable, valued, and respected.

- *Embrace a growth mindset:* In doing new kinds of work with new partners, it's almost guaranteed that you won't always know what you're doing. Don't be hard on yourself when you hit a snag or make a mistake; fix it and remember that your goal is to contin-

> ## Figure 4-2. The Implicit Association Test
>
> The Implicit Association Test (IAT) measures attitudes and beliefs that people may be unwilling or unable to report. The IAT may be especially interesting if it shows that you have an implicit attitude that you did not know about. For example, you may believe that women and men should be equally associated with science, but your automatic association could show that you (like many others) associated men with science more than women with science.
>
> *Source:* Project Implicit, https://implicit.harvard.edu/implicit/takeatest.html.

uously learn and improve in order to serve teens in the best way possible.

## Discover Your Community

Let's face it, libraries are often understaffed, filling any number of community needs, and just plain *busy*. Doing frontline library work can and usually does feel like a marathon. The work that libraries do is incredibly important, but in order to become even more efficient, thoughtful, and strategic about efforts, it's essential to build in time to test assumptions and learn about the community. Communities evolve, and in order to reflect this, libraries must continuously stay ahead of the curve.

As you begin your community discovery process, it's important to stay cognizant of the goals of the work. During this phase of the process, you are simply gathering information. You will be learning and testing assumptions about the populations that make up your community, the programs and services that are available, where young people spend their time, and potentially their high-level needs and aspirations. You are not actually designing new programs and services. This is an important distinction to make because as you learn and perhaps develop new relationships, it'll be tempting to roll up your sleeves and get started. Don't. The point of this process is to develop context that will inform your next steps and later support your facilitation with community members.

Inserting colleagues, existing volunteers, or teen advisory board members in your discovery process can be an extremely valuable part of the process. Not only will you be able to learn together, but a diverse per-

# Figure 4-3. Care about Community

Adapted from "Librarians as Community Ambassadors" by Shana Hinze, *YALS*, Fall 2016.

When I became a librarian at a teen tech space in an urban area, I decided to take a different approach. I performed all the expected outreach, but I also engaged in a more embedded approach. It was a time when gun violence in the library neighborhood was high, tensions were elevated, and we, as library staff, wanted to take an active role in working to change the situation. A colleague suggested taking outreach a step further and demonstrate our support by attending community events such as an anti-violence forum, as well as a wake, memorial, and funeral of young shooting victims.

When we attended the anti-violence event sponsored in part by the county, for example, we spoke to the crowd about impactful services for teens. One of our crowning services, as we mentioned, is a teen tech space, located conveniently in the neighborhood. It is equipped to teach filmmaking, photography, graphic design, coding, robotics, music production, and boasts Apple computers, professional-level software, and a future sound booth. Many people did not know the space existed and were glad to know the library system was investing in their youth with such resources.

Some of the teens from the space also attended the event and spoke about their experiences with gun violence as well as their positive experience at the library. Likewise, library staff involvement at the event served as a concrete example of our support for our teens who were affected by the violence. They saw us personally take an active role in the welfare of their lives while simultaneously modeling positive ways to engage their community. My coworker further declared that we were there to hear what the public needed. If there was a program or service they wanted, and we didn't offer it, we were listening. The message to the audience that evening was clear: The library truly cares about the people in our community. This was evident in the representation of library staff among other respected government personnel such as police officers, firefighters, teachers, and city and county commissioners.

You can do it too! Join groups; attend meetings; drop in at intergovernmental meetings, service clubs, parent-teacher meetings; reach out to the social services office, WIC office, state job placement office, schools, after-school programs. The idea is to go where people in the community go to get help, ask for things, or get things done. Becoming part of these groups will allow you to see and hear first-hand the needs of the community. Take a look at the organization listing at your local Chamber of Commerce, look up service organizations in your neighborhood, drive around town (you may find an organization that you didn't know existed or isn't published), contact churches and social services offices. You can make these types of community outreach activities work in your community. Don't be scared to get started. You'll find that it's well worth it.

spective and knowledge base will only improve the results. If you are new to this kind of a focus and including others feels like a challenge, think about how you can make community discovery a recurring theme in your practice with teens as you progress over time.

The easiest way to get started with community discovery is to know your numbers. Although data often carries its own biases, having a clear picture of basic statistics will give you a foundation and context from which to build on. It will also help you increase credibility with partners and administrators as you add other elements of your engagement process. With that in mind, stay cognizant of the various audiences that you might share information with, and record what you learn in such a way that it will be easily accessible to others.

Start with local school district information for your service area (this can be found with your State Department of Education or Superintendent of Public Instruction's website). Ask yourself:

- How many students are there?

- What is the racial/ethnic breakdown?

- What stands out to you in testing data?

- What do you notice about special programs?

- Is kindergarten-readiness data available?

- What are the graduation and college attendance rates?

- In which areas do you notice higher levels of chronic absenteeism or discipline problems?

- Do you see any trends?

- How does your district compare to overall state statistics?

- How does school district information relate to information about demographics from the overall community?

- How do your community demographics relate to regional or state-level data?

Once you feel comfortable with your basic landscape, explore issue-specific indicators through resources like Annie E. Casey Kids Count,[21] the Opportunity Index,[22] and if you are in a larger city, Measure of America.[23] Be sure to also be aware of local data as well that may be available through state or county agencies such as housing authorities or health districts.

The next phase in your community discovery process is to map the assets available to youth in your community and to assess needs. Asset mapping will give you a sense of the resources available to youth in your area. Not only will this activity help you connect young people and families within the library to resources, but it will also give you a sense of both strengths and opportunities for growth as you consider partnerships or design new services and initiatives. Assets are anything in your community that can be leveraged to improve the lives of teens. They can include public spaces such as parks where teens hang out, organizations that provide direct programs or services, businesses that appeal to teens or provide jobs, clubs at local schools, or even individuals to mentor teens.

While collecting raw data can be done in isolation, enlisting others to support these next few phases will greatly strengthen your efforts. This may be as simple as bringing a few colleagues on board or engaging an existing audience within the library to something more formal like recruiting a community advisory board made up of parents, providers, and teens. The latter would be especially beneficial if you are hoping to explore one specific community in your area, such as immigrant youth. Not only can others help you brainstorm and provide feedback on the process, but you'll likely benefit from diverse perspectives and experience, in addition to creating a broader network.

As you begin your asset mapping, think through all of the ways that you might collect this information:

- Drive or walk through neighborhoods. Where are people hanging out? How are they getting there? Are there spaces that could become assets?

- Survey county or city websites for organizations and providers.

- Call local schools to learn about available clubs. (If you don't yet know the office coordinator of your local school[s], you should!)

- Survey partners, youth, or community stakeholders in-person or online.

- Give cameras or an observation guide to a group of teens and ask them to document a specific period of time.

Once your information is collected, think about the best way to represent it in order to help you make connections. Can you group assets into broader categories (e.g., academic support, workforce development, safe spaces, basic needs)? Would a visual representation, such as a map, help you understand where services are clustered? Regardless of what you come up with, be sure to think about how to share this information with those who might benefit, including other after-school providers, social service agencies, or families.

In 2013, the Denver Public Library (DPL) went through an asset-mapping process. DPL is not the first library to participate in the teen assets-mapping process, but they are among the initial libraries to do so. In order to appropriately position DPL as a teen services provider, a team of DPL staff developed and implemented a project to identify and describe existing assets for teens in Denver, based on the Asset-Based Community Development model.

They developed and implemented a survey to ask service providers/

## Figure 4-4. What Is the Asset-Based Community Development Model?

Asset-Based Community Development (ABCD) is a strategy for sustainable community-driven development. Beyond the mobilization of a particular community, ABCD is concerned with how to link micro-assets to the macro-environment. The appeal of ABCD lies in its premise that communities can drive the development process themselves by identifying and mobilizing existing, but often-unrecognized assets, and thereby responding to and creating local economic opportunity.

ABCD builds on the assets that are already found in the community and mobilizes individuals, associations, and institutions to come together to build on their assets—not concentrate on their needs. An extensive period of time is spent in identifying the assets of individuals, associations, and then institutions before they are mobilized to work together to build on the identified assets of all involved. Then the identified assets from an individual are matched with people or groups who have an interest or need in that asset. The key is to begin to use what is already in the community.

*Source:* DePaul Asset-Based Community Development Institute, https://resources.depaul.edu/abcd-institute/about/Pages/default.aspx.

organizations to identify and describe what assets currently exist for teens. Part of the process was one-on-one phone calls and in-person interviews to find out more about services and programs provided for teens in Denver as well as the makeup of the community of teens. Historically, DPL didn't have teen services as part of the overall focus of the institution, and part of the teen asset mapping was to identify the teen community so to be able to better serve them in the library as well as identify other organizations that serve the age group.

The focus of the project was as follows:

- To identify and describe the way in which organizations in Denver supported teen assets.

- To identify themes and gaps in asset-based services in Denver.

- To understand how the library can work with community partners to develop asset-based teen services.

DPL identified forty-five organizations that work and serve teens. They connected with organizations through

- In-person interviews

- E-mail and phone calls

The asset-mapping team also surveyed 144 of the 435 staff at DPL to understand to what degree the staff is a teen asset. The survey questions were designed to capture general information as well as gauge the ways in which teens are or are not welcomed at DPL locations. The end product of the teen asset-mapping project helped the library to position itself effectively to expand library services for and with teens.

A needs assessment is just as valuable as asset mapping. Where asset mapping will provide you with an understanding of what's working, a needs assessment will help you think through areas for growth and opportunity. Needs assessments can be used in a variety of ways. For example, based on analysis and your asset mapping, you might have an idea for a type of program or service. In order to validate that idea, you might survey youth and their families to see if you are actually filling a priority need, solicit ideas of what the new service or program would look like, who should be involved, and if they would be likely to support that effort. In this case, you would end up with enough information to develop a basic road map. There might be other instances where you don't have a clear pathway to move forward with, and you're looking to build a more general understanding of community needs. In this case you might do the following:

- Interview other agencies or educators about the needs that they see, barriers that they face, and discuss areas for growth within the community;

- Facilitate focus groups or short interviews with youth and their families in the library or through partners, schools, or other youth organizations.

"Libraries Transforming Communities," a framework developed by the Harwood Institute for Public Innovation, is a great resource to help you do this.[24] Guided by training and a step-by-step process, facilitators are able to uncover the "aspirations" of a community through a series of formal and informal community conversations. From there, library staff reflect upon the implications of how those aspirations may impact their work and think about various ways to take action. Tools related to this model such as the "Intentionality" self-assessment exercise or the "Ask Exercise" facilitation guide could easily be woven into ongoing community engagement practice, regardless of whether you decide to move forward with the full process.

Design Thinking for Libraries, developed by IDEO, is another framework to help you move through both discovery and development processes.[25] With design thinking, facilitators think through a challenge, imagine possible solutions, then test and refine that solution. Because the core of design thinking is to consider and develop a solution to user needs, this process can easily be integrated into your community engagement strategy in both small ways, like designing a new program, and with very large projects, such as reorganizing organizational structure to support community engagement.

## Design

By now, learning and discovery have become a part of your regular practice. The time that you invested in preparation can now be used to design services and initiatives for and with community members. Depending on the scale of the initiative that you're working on and/or your position within the library, you may be working with one specific or cross-sector stakeholder group at various times. Consider the possibilities of "community" and who you might engage:

TEENS

Achieving true youth voice (see chapter 3 for more on this topic)—when young people are empowered to make meaningful decisions based upon their needs and interests—will in fact feel very reminiscent of the community engagement spectrum referenced at the beginning of this chapter. As with that spectrum, it will be important to continually take stock of your role in the process and to make adjustments to your role as support and facilitator.

## PARENTS

Although the parents of teens can sometimes seem like mythical creatures for the amount that you actually are able to see and connect with them, don't overlook the opportunity to engage them in your community engagement strategies. Not only can they be a major asset to learn from and in planning phases such as asset mapping and needs assessments; they can also help you reinforce skills and evaluate your efforts. Say, for example, you host a design thinking series with a partner organization to gather insight on what parents and teens would want in a new community center. Your secondary outcome is that you will have the opportunity to practice 21st-century skills, such as flexibility, problem solving, and teamwork, as a result of participating in the process. By asking both parents and teens to participate in the same activities, not only will participants learn from each other in the types of examples that each puts forward, but parents may increase their ability to see skill building in action, and therefore reinforce those concepts long after the program has ended. They could also offer valuable perspective on the outcomes of your program by speaking to how their child changed as a result of attending.

## COLLEAGUES

You might also think about internal colleagues as potential partners. If your library system has HR, finance and benefits, or administrative positions, think about how the people in those positions can support teens and your efforts with activities such as interview coaching, budgeting tips, or leadership chats.

## ORGANIZATIONS AND COMMUNITY MEMBERS

Organizations and community members are another important stakeholder group, offering different expertise, capacity, and networks. Typically, libraries think of these groups within the context of sharing frontline programming, but don't be afraid to think outside the box. For example, you might share training with other youth organizations in your area, collaborate on equipment lists, or simply discuss planning and curriculum. They can also be incredibly strong assets during needs assessment and planning. For example, say youth disconnection—the number of youth not working and not in school—is an increasing trend in your community. Including other organizations in these activities

# Figure 4-5. Case Study: Leadership Anchorage Leads to Collective Impact

Adapted from "Leadership Anchorage" by Stephanie Schott, *YALS*, Fall 2016

Leadership Anchorage (LA) started as one of ten national programs of the Pew Partnership for Civic Change in 1997. The program was embraced as a way to gain more diverse participants in city government and serving on boards and councils. In turn, these organizations would garner more input from and exposure to various cultural and ethnic groups. By the time Pew funding ended, LA was adopted and sustained through local financial support. With the guidance of the Alaska Humanities Forum, LA uses a humanities approach to study the cultural, political, and civic environment of Anchorage, Alaska, and the world. The program prides itself on recruiting established and emerging leaders from diverse backgrounds and professions. Together, each year's cohort experiences a two-day retreat, nine full-day Saturday sessions, one-on-one mentorship with a community leader, and discussions based on readings and the results of various personality tests, as well as spending over 80 hours working on a group project that benefits Anchorage.

Projects are solicited from the community to address specific needs and selected by LA members. Group projects included a workforce development program, Alaska fiscal education, a civic engagement academy, and citywide housing surveys. Following my passion for community engagement and planning, I joined the team working to set up a Farmers' Market in the Mountain View neighborhood. The project consisted of regular meetings with our two LA alumni liaisons, representatives from local organizations, and the project's champion, Anchorage Community Land Trust. It was my pleasure to work with Madonna, Raul, and Chandre. Our group was cemented with a contract that defined our goals, milestones, boundaries, and roles. We agreed to meet once a week to check in about our project, our LA experience, and our lives. This was to be the only time I worked in a group where each person was fully present and pulled his/her own weight. This dynamic made our tasks that much easier. Our group worked with project champions to craft a mission statement, reach out to other local markets for assistance, apply for EBT machines, get permits, buy equipment, create multiple lists and charts, establish an online and social media presence, contact vendors, and recruit volunteers. Everything came together despite losing our original location and starting with no seed money. Two of the most valuable pieces of this project for me were the involvement of the mayor's office and canvassing businesses in Mountain View. The mayor was still new to his post, and his office became interested in the LA program. A few key staff members were sent to work with us. At the first few Farmers' Market meetings, the mayor's representative was able to provide real assistance with permitting and information about other official requirements. Monthly meetings with the mayor's office with a representative from each of LA's groups provided a rare opportunity to receive suggestions for moving forward as well as a chance to have the ear of local government.

By canvassing the neighborhood, we had a great experience reaching out to the community. It was amazing to visit so many small businesses owned by first-generation and immigrant families. These conversations informed our team and guided our next steps. I have to say that this effort was my favorite part of the project because it was so mutually beneficial: extending personal welcomes to community members helped make the market something they could own, and increased word-of-mouth made the market that much more successful. The first ever Mountain View Farmers' Market opened on June 16, 2016.

will help you have a deeper understanding of the needs of your target demographic as well as a broader sense of the capacity available to address it.

COALITIONS OR COLLECTIVE IMPACT TEAMS

The final tier of your community stakeholder group is coalitions or collective impact teams. Rather than working in isolation, the goal of collective impact is to work toward shared goals with a strong structure in place for continuous learning and improvement. If you think about the partnerships on the continuum of community engagement, collective impact would be the highest level of partnership. All involved parties will have moved beyond collaborating and informing to become joint facilitators toward a shared outcome within the community. Needless

## Figure 4-6. Five Elements of Collective Impact

- All participants have a *common agenda* for change including a shared understanding of the problem and a joint approach to solving it through agreed-upon actions.

- Collecting data and *measuring results consistently* across all the participants ensures shared measurement for alignment and accountability.

- A plan of action that outlines and coordinates *mutually reinforcing activities* for each participant.

- Open and *continuous communication* is needed across the many players to build trust, assure mutual objectives, and create common motivation.

- A *backbone organisation(s)* with staff and specific set of skills to serve the entire initiative and coordinate participating organizations and agencies.

*Source:* Collaboration for Impact, "The Collective Impact Framework," http://www.collaborationforimpact.com/collective-impact/.

to say, collective impact requires the momentum of entire organizations, so it is a goal that cannot be achieved without buy-in from staff at all levels. That said, as you develop growing trust and deeper relationships with partners, think about collective impact as a possible long-term endgame. Who should be involved? How can you enlist the support of administrators? Is there a likely backbone or core team to move the work forward? The *Stanford Social Innovation Review* and the Collective Impact Forum are great sources to follow as you imagine the possibilities of collective impact in your community.

# Moving Forward

As you progress, it will be essential to plan for and reflect upon the community that you've brought together. Reserve plenty of time to think through and build skills related to the topics covered below. As you do, be sure to review resources like the Community Toolbox,[26] Design Thinking for Libraries,[27] Libraries Transforming Communities,[28] and the Tamarack Institute.[29] (You will find these and many others on the YALSA wiki.[30]) Each resource provides you with a wealth of tools, resources, and activities to support your learning and your process.

## Recruitment

Based on what you know about your community and the needs that you have discovered, do you have adequate representation? Based on your asset mapping, are there groups or individuals that you could connect with to extend a personal invitation to targeted groups? Can you clearly articulate the potential benefits of participating, both in terms of what various audiences might contribute and the issue that you might address together? Stakeholders, teen or adult, are much more likely to participate if they receive a personal invitation to do so and if they understand exactly what the benefit is to them and to the community if they do decide to participate.

## Facilitation

Consider your environment. Might there be barriers that would prevent participation by your intended community such as lack of transportation to location? If so, consider where you can host meetings and events so that those who don't have transportation options can still attend. Consider as well what infrastructure you will need to develop in order to guarantee that everyone feels welcome, safe, and supported. This may include instituting regular activities like icebreakers, reflection questions, jointly planned agendas, as well as discussing group norms, roles, and how you plan to communicate between meetings.

## Shared Goals

You've done your homework on data, assets, or aspirations, but was your stakeholder group involved in the process? Does everyone agree upon and have buy-in on the goals of your project and know where they fit into the solution? Make sure that the goals aren't simply designed to speak to what the library is trying to achieve. Focus on the goals of the entire community and all those who are a part of the designing and implementation process.

## Assessment and Evaluation

What are the outcomes that you hope to achieve? How are you collecting data that will help you improve your project or program? How will you know when you're successful or that your work is complete? Again, don't think just about the library when it comes to assessment and evaluation. Work with your partners to develop data measures that will help the entire community speak to the impact and value of the work. The more data you and your partners have, the better you will be able to tell your community story, and that will ultimately be beneficial when talking with community decision makers, elected officials, and funders.

## Conclusion

The underlying premise of community engagement is that we (libraries, individuals, communities) are better together. The process of learning, discovering, and preparing oneself to work with others will demand self-awareness and effort. Relationships and partnerships will need nurturing and flexibility. Both will require patience and capacity that you might not currently have. Make and advocate for that time. By doing so, not only will you be able to work with greater intention, but the impact that you will be able to achieve for teens will be far greater. All teens deserve a connected, supportive community, access to opportunity, and whole teams of champions at the ready to help them be successful in school, careers, and life. As YALSA's *Futures Report* encourages, "Be bold, persistent and critical. Do not be afraid to experiment. Above all, never lose sight of your goal: to change the lives of teens and provide them with a brighter future. In the end, you won't just be changing teens' lives—you'll be changing libraries and making them great!"[31]

## Notes

1.  Linda W. Braun, Maureen Hartman, Sandra Hughes-Hassell, and Kafi Kumasi, *The Future of Library Services for and with Teens: A Call to Action* (IMLS and YALSA, January 2014), http://www.ala.org/yaforum/sites/ala.org.yaforum/files/content/YALSA_nationalforum_final.pdf (accessed February 21, 2017).

2.  White House Council for Community Solutions, *Final Report: Community Solutions for Opportunity Youth*, June 2012, https://www.serve.gov/sites/default/files/ctools/12_0604whccs_finalreport.pdf (accessed February 22, 2017).

3.  "Community Engagement Assessment Tool," in *Building the Field of Community Engagement*, 2015, https://static1.squarespace.com/static/54317469e4b-056843fc6796c/t/553018e1e4b0389cde710c80/1429215457495/BTF-As-

sessYourWork.pdf (accessed February 22, 2017); White House Council for Community Solutions, *Final Report: Community Solutions for Opportunity Youth.*

4. U.S. Census Bureau, "Millennials Outnumber Baby Boomers and Are Far More Diverse," news release, June 25, 2015, http://www.census.gov/newsroom/press-releases/2015/cb15-113.html (accessed February 22, 2017).

5. Donald J. Hernandez and Wendy D. Cervantes, *Children in Immigrant Families: Ensuring Opportunity for Every Child in America* (First Focus, March 2011), https://firstfocus.org/wp-content/uploads/2014/06/Children-in-Immigrant-Families-Ensuring-Opportunity-for-Every-Child-in-America.pdf (accessed February 22, 2017).

6. Social Science Research Council, "Disconnected Youth," *Measure of America*, http://www.measureofamerica.org/disconnected-youth/ (accessed February 23, 2017).

7. Melinda D. Anderson, "Why Are So Many Preschoolers Getting Suspended," *The Atlantic*, December 7, 2015, https://www.theatlantic.com/education/archive/2015/12/why-are-so-many-preschoolers-getting-suspended/418932/ (accessed February 23, 2017).

8. Eileen Patten and Jens Manuel Krogstad, "Black Child Poverty Rate Holds Steady, Even as Other Groups See Declines," *Pew Research Center*, July 14, 2015, http://www.pewresearch.org/fact-tank/2015/07/14/black-child-poverty-rate-holds-steady-even-as-other-groups-see-declines/ (accessed February 23, 2017).

9. Joshua Rovner, *Racial Disparities in Youth Commitments and Arrests* (The Sentencing Project, April 1, 2016), http://www.sentencingproject.org/publications/racial-disparities-in-youth-commitments-and-arrests/ (accessed February 23, 2017).

10. Social Science Research Council, "Zeroing In on Place and Race," *Measure of America*, June 10, 2015, http://www.measureofamerica.org/youth-disconnection-2015/ (accessed February 23, 2017).

11. P. Carnavale, Tamara Jayasundera, and Artem Gulish, *America's Divided Recovery: College Haves and Have-Nots 2016* (Center on Education and the Workforce, Georgetown University, 2016), https://cew.georgetown.edu/wp-content/uploads/Americas-Divided-Recovery-web.pdf (accessed February 23, 2017).

12. U.S. Bureau of Labor Statistics, "STEM 101: Intro to Tomorrow's Jobs," *Occupational Outlook Quarterly*, Spring 2014, https://www.bls.gov/careeroutlook/2014/spring/art01.pdf (accessed February 23, 2017).

13. Youth Truth, "Learning from Student Voice: College and Career Readiness," http://www.youthtruthsurvey.org/college-and-career-readiness/ (accessed April 12, 2017).

14. Common Sense, *The Common Sense Census: Media Use by Tweens and Teens*, 2015, https://www.commonsensemedia.org/sites/default/files/uploads/research/census_researchreport.pdf (accessed February 23, 2017).

15. Melody Barnes and Paul Schmitz, "Community Engagement Matters (Now More than Ever)," *Stanford Social Innovation Review*, Spring 2016, https://ssir.org/articles/entry/community_engagement_matters_now_more_than_ever (accessed February 23, 2017).

16. bell hooks, *Teaching Community: A Pedagogy of Hope* (New York: Routledge, 2003).

17. American Library Association, Office for Diversity, Literacy, and Outreach Service, "Diversity Counts," September 19, 2012, http://www.ala.org/offices/diversity/diversitycounts/divcounts (accessed February 23, 2017).

18. National Center for Education Statistics, "Status and Trends in the Education of Racial and Ethnic Groups: Degrees Awarded," https://nces.ed.gov/programs/raceindicators/indicator_ree.asp (accessed April 13, 2017).

19. "On Racism and White Privilege," *Teaching Tolerance*, excerpted from Jennifer R. Holladay, *White Anti-Racist Activism: A Personal Roadmap* (2000), http://www.tolerance.org/article/racism-and-white-privilege (accessed February 23, 2017).

20. Peggy McIntosh, "White Privilege: Unpacking the Invisible Knapsack" and "Some Notes for Facilitators," National SEED Project, 1989, https://nationalseedproject.org/white-privilege-unpacking-the-invisible-knapsack (accessed February 23, 2017).

21. Annie E. Casey Foundation, "Kids Count," http://www.aecf.org/work/kidscount/ (accessed February 23, 2017).

22. Opportunity Index, "How Opportunity Measures Up in Your Community," http://opportunityindex.org/#4.00/40.00/-97.00/ (accessed February 23, 2017).

23. Measure of America of the Social Science Research Council, http://www.measureofamerica.org/ (accessed February 23, 2017).

24. American Library Association, "Libraries Transforming Communities," Libraries Transform, February 14, 2017, http://www.ala.org/transforminglibraries/libraries-transforming-communities (accessed February 23, 2017).

25. IDEO, *Design Thinking for Libraries*, http://designthinkingforlibraries.com/ (accessed February 23, 2017).

26. Work Group for Community Health and Development at the University of Kansas, "Table of Contents," Community Tool Box, 2016, http://ctb.ku.edu/en/table-of-contents (accessed February 23, 2017).

27. IDEO, *Design Thinking for Libraries*, http://designthinkingforlibraries.com/

(accessed February 23, 2017).

28. American Library Association, "Libraries Transforming Communities," Libraries Transform, February 14, 2017, http://www.ala.org/transforminglibraries/libraries-transforming-communities (accessed February 23, 2017).

29. Tamarack Institute, "Community Engagement," http://www.tamarackcommunity.ca/communityengagement (accessed February 23, 2017).

30. Young Adult Library Services Association, "YALSA Wiki," http://wikis.ala.org/yalsa/index.php/Main_Page (accessed February 23, 2017).

31. Braun et al., *The Future of Library Services for and with Teens*.

CABELL COUNTY PUBLIC LIBRARY (WV)

# Summer Teen Interns

BREANA ROACH BOWEN

## What Did You Want to Achieve?

At the Cabell County Public Library we wanted our summer teen interns to:

- Understand the hierarchy of the workplace. Specifically, what it means to be an employee reporting to a manager.

- Learn about being a part of a team and working together to achieve goals and objectives, ultimately building strong and supportive relationships with peers and adults.

- Have experience in making their own decisions.

- Know that it's okay to make mistakes and try new things. We wanted to empower our teens through education,

- Be motivated individuals who gained confidence, resiliency, and learned to trust themselves as individuals who are capable of giving back to their community and bettering themselves.

## Overview of the Program/Project

Every summer, as a part of our system-wide summer reading program, The Cabell County Public Library hosts a Super Why reading camp. This program is held in partnership with our local PBS station and the camp is designed to help preschool age children learn to read. Traditionally, we have teens help with the program. This year, we were fortunate enough to be the recipients of a YALSA and Dollar General Literacy Foundation Summer Teen Intern Grant.  As a result we had the funds to hire eight paid teen interns.

These interns assisted library staff at the camps. The teens worked with the small children in a variety of activities ranging from helping with technology to supporting daily reading activities. We also were able to have our teen interns help with a variety of other youth services programs. For example, they helped children sign-up for summer reading, helped to host programs, worked with staff in creating and implementing craft activities and helped serve free lunch. When the internship was complete, every participating teen received a stipend.

## What Challenges Did You Face and How Did You Overcome Them?

We really did not face any challenges. Our teen intern program ran pretty smoothly; however, if we are given this opportunity again it would be nice to expand the program outside of our Super Why Reading Camps and allow the teens more opportunities to help with our Summer Reading Program. This would allow the teens to gain more diverse, hands-on experience working with the community and families. The teens would be able to reach a larger portion of our library demographic, ultimately learning more about our community.

## What Did You Learn?

We learned so much from having a teen intern program! This program enabled our library system to reach our teen demographic like we have never been able to before. We learned that many teens in our community are looking for volunteer and internship opportunities to gain crucial skills needed to thrive outside of high school. We realized there is a significant need for teen volunteer positions within our community. The teens were able to learn about library staff and our profession, and we were able to better ourselves and our organization from working with the teens.

## How Does This Work Connect to YALSA's Futures Report and Vision?

Our program connected to YALSA's Futures Report and Vision on many different levels. For example, teen interns were able to:

- Learn, work in leadership roles, build a sense of community, and explore their creativity.

- Gain critical skills needed to enter the workforce.

- Participate in workforce development training through real-world experiences.

- Explore careers in library settings.

- Connect with adult mentors (library staff) and learn through real-life experience.

- Make decisions and become more independent individuals.

- Be a part of a team that worked together to achieve goals and objectives, ultimately building strong and supportive relationships with peers and adults.

Ultimately, our teens were empowered through education, and they gained confidence, resiliency, and learned to trust themselves as individuals who are capable of giving back to their community and bettering themselves.

One of our interns has been volunteering at the library for years. He was the summer teen intern at the Main Library over the summer. He told library staff that he has decided to pursue a career in early child-hood education because of the program. It is wonderful knowing that the library and internship program had such a positive impact on this young man and his future career plans!

The most important thing to come out of this program was that the teens were able to build lasting and crucial relationships with the adult library staff. Many of the interns have continued to visit the library, and the teens and their parents would like to see the program continued in the future. Overall, the program was highly successful and allowed us to do our part to help the teens lead successful and fulfilling lives.

# CHAPTER 5

# Assessments and Outcome-Based Evaluation in Formal and Informal Learning Spaces

AMANDA WAUGH, NATALIE GREENE TAYLOR, AND KELLY HOFFMAN

For the past decade, youth informal learning and formal education have been in a state of flux. From shifts in the tools used in these environments (e.g., iPads, SMART Boards, and laptops)[1] to the very skills young people want and need to learn (e.g., information, technology, and media skills, such as understanding ethical and legal issues related to the use of technology and the ability to create media products using the most relevant tools).[2] As a result, the adults working with youth are making changes in their practices of teaching and facilitation. As the executive summary of the report *The Future Library Services for and with Teens: A Call to Action* states:

> In order to meet the needs of today's teens and to continue to provide value to their communities, libraries need to revisit their fundamental structure, including these components: audience; collections; space; programming; staffing; youth participation; outreach; policy; professional development.[3]

Fundamental to these changes is an understanding of the impact of library activities for teens on teens. In other words, both formal and informal educators are increasingly focusing on outcomes, "clear learning results that we want students to demonstrate at the end of significant learning experiences."[4] This is of course not an entirely new phenomenon. Any good educator is used to evaluating his or her personal performance and using a trained eye to see whether a program or lesson has been effective or not. What perhaps has changed, or at least increased, is an intentional focus on outcomes through formal assessment processes to demonstrate the value of a library activity and/or staff member's existence. Increasingly, libraries and other informal learning environments are required to demonstrate value and funding need through sophisticated data. Attendance or circulation numbers are no longer enough; there must be some evidence of impact on the participant.

While this chapter is primarily written for library staff serving teens in school and public libraries, educators and researchers interested in or involved with teens can benefit from the ideas presented. We explore both the ways and means of outcomes assessment in school and public libraries.

This chapter is structured into three sections. First, we look at how outcomes and learning are connected. Then we describe practical steps to performing outcome-based evaluation in different environments and using different methods. The third section looks at different types of learning frameworks and how outcomes can be used to assess learning within those. Throughout these sections, we highlight various case studies to show how evaluation might look outside the context of a research environment. It is our goal to take away the stigma from the term "evaluation." By drawing on our personal experience with youth, educators, researchers, and funding agencies, we shed light on ways one can evaluate in a way that embraces a youth's interest in learning and an educator's desire to foster interest-based learning experiences.

# Outcomes and Learning

In the age of testing and standardization, "outcomes" and "evaluation" are often seen as loaded terms. Although certainly not always the case, informal learning spaces tend toward more informal assessments, while formal learning spaces are associated with more formal assessments. Some of the reasons for this are discussed below; we also want to make it clear that this is not always the case (nor should it be). There is plenty of informal learning going on in school libraries and, sometimes by necessity, formal evaluations taking place in the public library. Examples of this are included throughout the rest of this chapter. First however, what are outcomes?

Traditionally, in a formal educational space, such as a school, learning has been the key outcome sought. In an informal environment, such as a public library, fun was often the key outcome without much notice of whether or not that fun led to some sort of specific change in knowledge, behavior, skills, or attitude. What we now know, is that the ability to speak the "language" of those two environments, or melding "fun" with learning, will allow libraries of all types to achieve greater impact for and with youth and by extension, in communities. Take for example a program in which teens are engaged in group games and icebreakers. From the outside, this may just seem like fun, but those activities are in fact leading to a short term outcome of building community with a new target audience. As a result of feeling more comfortable and confident with peers and facilitators, teens will have the confidence to engage in learning a new skill, which is an appropriate as a mid-level outcome.

When planning a program and an evaluation of that program, consider the desired impact on the audience of the activity and how these might be scaffolded during your activity and over time. The Institute of Museum and Library Services (IMLS) defines outcome-based evaluation as "a series of services or activities that lead towards observable, intended changes for participants."[5] The following are potential outcomes of any type of learning space—formal or informal:

- Confidence

- Enthusiasm towards learning

- Attainment of skills

- Improvement in various literacies (e.g., information, health, science)

- Understanding of the value of learning and a desire to pursue future learning/career pathways

From a funder, stakeholder, or decision-maker perspective, outcomes may also be rooted in a focus on return on investment (ROI). ROI is an increasingly popular way of making decisions regarding funding allocation. A study by the Library Research Service defines ROI by a value that "demonstrates the worth of public libraries in terms of dollars-and-cents," and this is indeed typically the framework within which

ROI is measured.[6] In its most basic terms, ROI is getting one's money's worth. Value is certainly demonstrated in other ways as well. For example, positive public perception might be an additional outcome—and one that could have powerful impact on the aforementioned funders. The ability to effectively communicate outcomes will enable library staff to move beyond the "numbers game" for youth library programs and shift toward impact. In future-focused teen library service, one well-developed story of personal change is more meaningful than large attendance any day.

# Steps to Planning a Successful Outcome-Based Evaluation or Assessment

Below are manageable, ordered steps for developing an outcome-based evaluation. It's important to know that the process of evaluation and outcomes is not always clean or linear. Similarly, not all activities are right for an evaluation of this type. The areas covered include the following:

- Assess the situation.

- Know your audience.

- Understand your goals.

- Design the instrument.

- Administer the assessment.

- Interpret the assessment.

- Decide where and how to distribute your findings.

## Step One: Assess the Situation

The first step is to assess the situation to determine if your project is right for an outcome-based evaluation (OBE), as described by the New York State Library. Although this type of evaluation can certainly be done without all the following prerequisites, OBE works best when your project

- "Is designed for a clearly defined audience

- Addresses specific needs of that audience

- Provides a variety of activities to address the need

- Provides for repeated contacts or follow-up with the target audience

- Is designed for the target audience to acquire new or improved skills, knowledge, attitudes or behaviors that are *attitudes or behaviors that are predictable and measurable.*"[7]

You should also consider your location (e.g., public or school library), the length of the program (is it long term or a one-off?), and your audience. Understanding these issues can help you to figure out what resources you may need to begin the evaluation, ways the program may need to be tweaked to fit an assessment model, and the timeline you have for pursuing the research. Ask yourself the following questions:

1. Is someone asking you to perform the outcome-based assessment for their own purpose, or is this aimed primarily for improvement in future programs?

2. Are you interested in performing periodic assessments throughout a program or simply after the program is completed? Can you follow up with participants after more time has passed?

3. How will you handle retention (or lack thereof)? In other words, in an ongoing program, what will you do if a participant misses occasional sessions?

4. What are your resources? Do you have funding to provide incentives for participation? Do you have money for recording devices or printing and design of tools? Perhaps most importantly, within what time constraints are you working?

5. What do your participants know already? Will you need to teach skills related to your primary goals for the participants to successfully complete the program? (This is common when teaching skills related to technology; sometimes teaching the tool takes as much time as the content).

# Figure 5-1. Case Study: Observations from a School Library Administrator

The evaluation process I participated in as a school librarian was at times confusing. In my district, we are called media specialists and, at that time, were evaluated under a similar, but not identical, process to classroom teachers. Outcomes should be a critical component of the evaluation process—in this case, demonstrating that the students had learned the skill or information that was the goal of the lesson.

Media specialists developed a lesson plan using a specific and very detailed format, which was designed to ensure that the school librarian was considering all the needs of their students and examining their instructional practices to promote learning. Aspects included a detailed outline of how the lesson would be accessible to different learners, such as struggling students, English-language learners, and those identified as Talented and Gifted. Effective plans also included classroom management strategies and alternative assessments.

The plan required specifying the objective for the lesson, each step of the lesson, the resources required to teach it, the media specialist's self-reflective practices at each stage, the standards being taught, and the related assessment for student learning. While the term "outcome-based evaluation" was not used, that is what we were doing. We met with the evaluator (typically the principal or the assistant principal) to review the lesson and to explain the strategies and assessments. The focus of this process was demonstrating that the educator had planned assessments that would adequately capture the outcomes expected from the lesson.

It's important in this type of process that understanding the language the administrator used was critical to a successful evaluation. After all, the administrator is steeped in a certain perspective. When the educator translates their assessment methods, objectives, and anticipated outcomes into the administrator's perspective, they are much more likely to be well received.

Following this meeting, media specialists were observed. The observation required the lesson to be at least 30 minutes. For my purposes, the challenge was to include both a lesson that met the needs of the evaluation process and that allowed students time to check out books—which was their favorite part—in a lesson period that was often not much more than 30 minutes. I was able to make this work by building relationships with classroom teachers who allowed me to keep a class a bit longer than normal or would bring their classes at a different time for a quick visit to circulate books.

After the observation, I met with the principal or assistant principal to review the lesson and present the assessment results. Obviously, we all wanted to show an effective lesson and positive assessments, but I found it is always important to also reflect on areas for improvement.

6. How will you handle different learning styles and abilities? Will you include goals that allow for participants with less experience to successfully achieve the program's intended results? What about participants who have prior knowledge of the content?

7. What is your organization's policy on collecting data? When working with minors, consent and privacy considerations are paramount. What are the consent and confidentiality parameters you are working within?

## Step Two: Understand Your Goals

To accurately measure anything, you must first articulate what results you are hoping the experience achieves. In other words, what should the participants gain or learn from the activity? This is perhaps the most important question within all the steps of the evaluation process. You must determine clear and measurable objectives and goals that you hope to achieve with a program, lesson, or service. Outcomes may vary widely from the acquisition of a skill, to the enthusiasm the participants express at the beginning and end of the program, to retention of participants. Typically, outcomes are expressed as a sentence describing what you hope to see when the program is complete. Outcomes are often written using the ABCD format: audience, behavior, conditions, and degree.[8] For example:

• When instructed on new databases (C), 75% (D) of teen program attendees (A) will be able to find an article (B) about a topic of personal interest.

- When introduced to the paper circuit program (C), two-thirds (D) of teens (A) will be able to explain how they were able to get their LED light to work (B).

- When participating in a ten-week program at the library's maker-space (C), 90% (D) of teen attendees (A) successfully articulated what they learned at the library's makerspace fair held at the end of the program (B).

While this technique is frequently employed in education settings, it also has a lot of merit in more informal settings because it requires thinking very carefully about what the goal is and being very specific about the impact that the experience is expected to achieve. It is also a great way to get started with outcomes because the formula allows you simply to insert the elements of the program, the results you are working toward, and your intended participants.

## Step Three: Design the Evaluation Tools and Implement Your Program

Designing the instrument should not occur in isolation from the planning of your program or lesson. In some cases, you may need to alter the plan you have in mind (to allow time for the assessment to be administered), your budget (to pay for resources needed to conduct the assessment), your outcomes (to ensure they are measurable given the type of assessment you are prepared to administer), or the preparation for the instructor (to train him or her on the assessment strategy). In addition, how you will use the analysis once it is completed will also guide the method of data collection you choose.

The chart below explores common types of data-gathering methods that might be used in assessing outcomes and when it is most appropriate to use the strategy. For more information, consult the New York State Library's "Outcome-Based Evaluation: Training Manuals,"[9] particularly the section on data sources, as well as the publication by the Forum for Youth Investment on measuring youth program outcomes.[10]

**Figure 5-2. Data-Gathering Techniques**

| Type of Assessment | When to Use | How to Implement | Example | Limitations |
|---|---|---|---|---|
| Observations are made by facilitators during a learning session by taking careful notes of how the participants are acting and what they seem to be learning or not. | Observations are best used to evaluate outcomes as the program is still going on to make changes that might be necessary to achieve the intended outcomes. | Frequently, the best way to get good observations from facilitators is to design a protocol of the specific behaviors for which to be looking. Facilitators should take notes during the session and, perhaps more critically, should go back and review these notes immediately after the learning session to contextualize the observations. | Goal: Through creation of e-textiles, teens are able to make a circuit work and overcome challenges along the way. Example: Facilitators note participants' actions during the activity. These might take the form of verbal responses or physical reactions, such as signs of frustration, annoyance, boredom, excitement, or attentiveness. | Observations can be hard to use as formal evaluations, as they can end up being subjective instead of objective without training and careful protocol development. |

| Type of Assessment | When to Use | How to Implement | Example | Limitations |
|---|---|---|---|---|
| A portfolio is a collection of assembled learning artifacts created by a participant over the course of the learning session. | Portfolios work best when they are used as part of an ongoing program (multiple sessions) where participants have opportunity to build a body of work. They can be used to show visually what participants have learned. | To successfully implement portfolio evaluations, the facilitator must provide guidelines to participants on what type of work is expected, suggest a place for participants to collect their materials (online or as hard copies), and clearly tie each artifact to a learning goal. | Goal: Participants will demonstrate understanding of STEAM (science, technology, engineering, arts, and math) concepts and competence in one STEAM domain. Example: A participant in a public library program produces a short animated video and shares an online portfolio demonstrating the versions and steps (storyboard, script, drawings, etc.) that led up to the final product. | Using portfolios for evaluation can mean an increased workload. Because many artifacts are used in the assessment, this creates more work in reviewing on behalf of the facilitator. Additionally, some may claim that evaluations are open to interpretation. To mitigate these weaknesses, Emma McDonald suggests identifying the purpose of the portfolio, developing a rating system to evaluate the portfolio (one could also use a rubric), and asking a colleague to review the work to ensure a lack of bias. |

| Pre- and post-tests ask participants the same (or very similar) questions at the beginning and end of the program. | This tool is best used when measurable data is needed; for example, when you want to see specific percentages of improvement for specific skills. | The most critical step in designing a pre- and post-test is to make sure the questions match your goals. If you are looking to see evidence of learning, your questions will need to ask the participant to demonstrate evidence of the learned skill. Additionally, pre-tests should be administered before any instruction takes place and post-tests should be administered after the activity for which you are attempting to evaluate efficacy. | Goal: Participants in the Intro to Technology library program will be able to articulate the difference between a ".com" website and a ".gov" website on a quiz by the end of the first session. Example: What is the difference between a ".com" website and a ".gov" website? | One important limitation of pre- and post-tests that are administered over a period of time is that you must consider intervening variables that might affect the outcome of the program. For example, did the participants engage in other lessons or activities that might have contributed to success or failure? What was the time interval between the tests? To mitigate these interferences, you can ask participants about their activities between the tests (e.g., did you learn anything about this subject in school/at home since last session?); or you can attempt to keep questions very specifically oriented toward the program (e.g., asking a question that specifically relates to an activity conducted during the program). |
| --- | --- | --- | --- | --- |

| Type of Assessment | When to Use | How to Implement | Example | Limitations |
|---|---|---|---|---|
| Surveys ask participants questions designed to understand their evaluations or opinions about activities, subjects, or feelings. | If you are trying to see a change in behavior, perception, or attitude, you'll want to ask questions pertaining to feelings or emotions. Attitudinal questions are often structured with a rating scale (e.g., asking to answer the question from "strongly agree" to "disagree"). | Designing survey questions requires the writer to be specific about what he or she is asking, to avoid attempting to guide the participant toward one answer or another, and to resist asking about multiple things within one question. Surveys can be administered at the beginning or the end of the learning activity. If you desire to see if there is a change over time, you should give the survey at both times. | Goal: Participants will indicate at the last session that they feel more pleasure from reading during their free time after participating in the library's summer learning book club. Example: On a scale of 1 to 5, with 1 representing strongly dislike, 2 representing dislike, 3 representing neutral, 4 representing like, and 5 representing strongly like, how much would you say you like spending time reading for pleasure? | Three common limitations of surveys are response fatigue, low response rates, and biased questions. Response fatigue occurs when a participant has either been asked to take the survey too frequently or the survey asks too many questions. This can be mitigated by being very judicious in what you are trying to ask. Response rates are generally less of a problem when the survey is administered in person, but could be an issue if you want to send surveys out to participants long after the program to gauge retention of change. Ensuring that the participant understands the importance of the research can help. Finally, biased questions can be avoided by having another reader review the survey. |

| | | | | |
|---|---|---|---|---|
| Focus groups are planned discussions between participants and a facilitator wherein the facilitator asks questions about the program and the learning that (hopefully) took place. | Focus groups are ideal for getting rich data in the form of quotes and unexpected results and when looking for participants to respond to each other and expand on one another's comments. | Focus group questions should be focused enough to clearly relate to your goal, but open-ended enough to prompt discussion and feedback. You will want to avoid asking yes or no questions, be willing to follow up and rephrase if a question produces little engagement, and be careful not to ask leading questions (e.g., Why did you like this program?). | Goal: Through creation of e-textiles teens are able to articulate what makes a circuit work or not work.<br><br>Example: What challenges did you face when working with the e-textile circuits and how did you get beyond them? | Careful conversation management must be employed to avoid the louder participants from drowning out the quieter participants. "Crowd control" is not what you would think would be the major job of the interviewer; but it is necessary and often critical to getting responses from the whole group. Depending on your group, the conversation can quickly go off-topic. You must be able to gently guide participants back on track. Finally, if the information you are discussing is sensitive, participants may be unwilling to share their true thoughts in front of a group (or the facilitator). This can be mitigated by creating a "safe space" for participants and by employing a facilitator who the participants feel comfortable with (but not one who they will be wary of disappointing through negative answers). |

Perhaps the most important part of implementation for focus groups is ensuring you take good notes and record the session. You will want to transcribe the audio after—you won't remember everything that was said! This requires considering issues of consent (formally in the case of university researchers through the Institutional Review Board). Most organizations have formal policies for these occasions.

| Type of Assessment | When to Use | How to Implement | Example | Limitations |
|---|---|---|---|---|
| Badges are visual representations of a skill achieved given to participants after demonstrating competence. | Often attached to gamification, badging offers an interactive way of showing knowledge, skill, or understanding. Badges are useful to use when steps in learning needs to be shown to others and digital artifacts help support that effort. | Badge platforms such as Credly provide facilitators the chance to connect specific learning modules to artifacts that learners create. These platforms require posting the learning plan or curriculum on the site and providing opportunity for learners to post their materials to the same site for evaluation and badge awarding. | As the Center for the Future of Libraries highlights, many public and school libraries have created their own form of badges for summer reading programs (e.g., Loveland Public Library in Colorado: http://loveland.readsquared.com/) and for meeting Common Core standards (e.g., New Milford High School in Connecticut: http://www.worlds-of-learning-nmhs.com/about/). | Badging requires buy-in from participants to work. If the participants do not care about the badge, it will not work as a motivating factor. Additionally, the badge movement has not caught on as any kind of official way of showing skills earned, so evaluation is limited to the individual institution running the learning activity. Even with badges, the learning facilitator needs to carefully consider evaluation and how that will be accomplished within the badging platform. |

# Figure 5-3. Case Study: Focus Groups in an Informal Learning Space

*HackHealth* was a weekly after-school program run in five middle schools in the mid-Atlantic during the 2013–14 and 2014–15 school years. Researchers and school librarians worked with participating teens for one to two hours per week for eight to 12 weeks. The focus of the work was on improving teen health and information literacy skills.

*HackHealth* was a pilot project with a focus on learning how best to facilitate youth investigations of personally relevant health issues, while simultaneously teaching information literacy skills and increasing individual self-efficacy. Although the project was local, the goal of the project was to provide insight on methods of teaching for replication nationwide. Because of the nature of the project, a designed-based strategy proved most useful; the school librarians and teens provided informal and formal feedback throughout the program, which enabled researchers to make changes in teaching in current and subsequent sessions.

Although the design-based research program included many assessments throughout, one of the most useful included focus groups with both the participating teens and their parents. The focus groups were designed as a natural outcrop of this design-based strategy and had the aim of gathering, from the students, thoughts about the program, favorite memories, how they described the program to friends, whether they would recommend the program to friends, the benefits they found in participating, and suggestions they had for improvement. Parents were asked about their "thoughts about the program, whether they would recommend [the program] to other parents, what [their] child got out of program, [whether] participating [was] helpful . . . , and suggestions for improvement."[1] Participants were asked about what they learned during the program and their answers, which included knowledge gained about website credibility and finding relevant health information, demonstrated success toward the program's goal to increase the participants' health and information literacy skills.

Focus groups were held at end-of-program celebrations for each school (except for one of the second year's celebration, which included three of the schools at one event). In addition to the focus groups, the researchers provided food for the participants and their families and the participants presented on what they learned throughout the program. These additions provided incentives for the participants to participate. Additionally, the focus groups were held at a local state university, which was a huge draw for this age group.

The only complications that arose during these groups were the need for translation for some of the parents (researchers found the interactions were more stilted because of the need to halt the natural flow of conversation) and the inevitable talkative participant who might prevent quieter members from speaking. Overall, however, the rewards far outweighed the troubles that arose. For more information on some of the feedback the program received, see hackhealth.umd.edu.

1. Beth St. Jean, Natalie Greene Taylor, Christie Kodama, Mega Subramaniam and Dana Casciotti, "Impacts of the *HackHealth* After-School Program: Motivating Youth through Personal Relevance," Wiley Online Library, 2015, http://onlinelibrary.wiley.com/doi/10.1002/pra2.2015.145052010032/epdf (accessed February 23, 2017), p. 3.

## Step Four: Interpreting the Assessment and Reporting Your Findings

After implementation, it is time to use the data to evaluate whether the participants in your program successfully met the intended goals. Again, this step is dependent on the tool used. Interpreting the assessment can be as complicated as performing statistical analysis or intricate qualitative data analysis, or as simple as reporting the feedback given on a survey or reports from participants on what they learned. For the tools described above, the biggest investment you will need to make in the analysis process is time. The pre- and post-tests and surveys will need to be compared and tallied. Notes from focus groups and observations, as well as session transcriptions, will need to be reviewed to find common themes relating to the goals of the program. Portfolios will need to be assessed against a rubric or scoring system, and the work will have to be viewed as a whole to see how successful the learning session was for the whole group. Badges will need to be assigned after student work has been graded or assessed.

How to report this data and how to present your analysis circles back

# Figure 5-4. YOUmedia

YOUmedia Chicago may be the most well-known implementation of connected learning in a public library. Founded in 2009 by the Digital Youth Network and the Chicago Public Library (CPL), with support from the MacArthur Foundation's Digital Media and Learning initiative, it was the first library space to put the HOMAGO (Hanging Out, Messing Around, Geeking Out) principles into practice.

To evaluate the newly developed initiative, CPL partnered with the University of Chicago Consortium on Chicago School Research for the first three years of YOUmedia's operation. Since this was an untested approach, the evaluation had the broader goal of examining whether it was effective and what design changes could be made to the model to make it better. Thus, the evaluative effort was designed to evaluate not only the impact that YOUmedia had on the teens, but also how internal forces and design choices may have impacted the outcomes.

Initially, the researchers' jobs were complicated by the breadth of the outcomes articulated by the program leaders, such as "being able to adapt to different ways to communicate, ways to explore, ways to research, ways to express yourself."[1] The first year of study involved unstructured observations and both structured and unstructured interviews with staff, teens, and YOUmedia leadership. It also included an evaluation of the online space created for YOUmedia, iRemix, where teens were encouraged to share their work and give feedback to each other. The year one report focused on the importance of the relationships between staff members and teens, the sense of community growing among teens who used the space, and the dynamic learning environment.[2] They also identified challenges to the model, like communication difficulties and the low usage of iRemix.

The first year's report helped define the research conducted over the remainder of the study. The researchers were able to articulate several research questions designed to uncover who was coming to YOUmedia, what benefits they saw from participating, and what changes to the program might help YOUmedia and other learning labs better achieve their goals. These research questions drove the evaluation activities conducted in the second and third years of the YOUmedia project.[3]

The unstructured observations and interviews continued in years two and three, with the addition of several other evaluation methods. They conducted surveys of youth and selected some to participate in case studies that followed them over the course of 15 months. They also performed two censuses of teens in the space, counting how many visited and asking them to complete a short anonymous paper-based or online questionnaire. The three-year report contains detailed descriptions of the research activities.[4]

The YOUmedia approach to evaluation continues to evolve. In 2012 the Institute of Museum and Library Services (IMLS) and the MacArthur Foundation partnered to offer grants to create several learning labs based on the YOUmedia model in museums and libraries. The "YOUmedia libraries" have formed an active community of practice, sharing ideas and lessons learned through webinars, Google Hangouts, and discussion boards.[5] One community member, Sara Ryan of Multnomah County Public Library, is developing outcome evaluation methods designed around the hallmark concepts.[6] For each concept—such as "Strive for a balance of hanging out, messing around, and geeking out"—she asks the question: "What does a successful implementation of this hallmark look like?" The answers include statements like "Youth choose to visit the space regularly" or "Youth feel that the space is welcoming." Ryan identifies practical yet creative ways to measure those elements—a badging system to reward check-ins can track regulars, and youth can express their feelings about the space or a program through emojis or gifs. The goal of measuring these outcomes is to "tell the story of your program"—to inspire funders, encourage and reward staff, or identify areas that need improvement.

1. Kimberly Austin, Stacy B. Ehrlich, Cassidy Puckett, and Judi Singleton, *YOUmedia Chicago: Reimagining Learning, Literacies, and Libraries: A Snapshot of Year 1* (Consortium on Chicago School Research, May 2011), http://consortium.uchicago. edu/downloads/6899youmedia_final_2011.pdf (accessed February 23, 2017).

2. Ibid.

3. Penny A. Sebring, Eric R. Brown, Kate M. Julian, Stacy B. Ehrlich, Susan E. Sporte, Erin Bradley, and Lisa Meyer, *Teens, Digital Media, and the Chicago Public Library* (Chicago: University of Chicago Consortium on Chicago School Research, 2013).

4. Ibid.

5. YOUmedia Network: Reimagining Learning in the 21st Century, http://youmedia. org/ (accessed February 23, 2017).

6. Sara Ryan, "Tell the Story: Use Outcomes to Show the Difference Your Program Makes," *Young Adult Library Services* (YALS) 12, no. 1 (Fall 2013): 13–15.

around to the question of intent. Why the data collection was carried out will directly impact your reporting style. If the evaluations were completed to assess the facilitation and program style to plan future activities, internal memos and notes about what needs to be improved is likely sufficient. If outsiders requested the data, more formal write-ups and/or visualizations may be necessary. Policymakers tend to appreciate brief visually appealing write-ups of the program, intended outcomes, analysis, and results. Politicians, on the other hand, are often most persuaded by personal stories they can report back to their constituents. Funders, future participants, the decision makers in your own organization, yourself (for personal reflection), parents, other organizations interested in replicating your program, and your community are all potential stakeholders, and you'll want to consider how you package your results to best appeal to each group. Sarah Ann Murphy created materials with details on how visually presenting data is useful to libraries,[11] while the online tools Infogram (https://infogr.am/) and Piktochart (https://piktochart.com/) are examples of free or low-cost programs available to help you create visuals for infographics or visual representations of data. The Ready by 21 organization links to several ways of using data in planning and accountability.[12]

## Evaluating through Formative and Summative Assessment

Formative assessments are intended to help a teacher or librarian in partnership with a student understand if learning is happening while an activity or a unit is in progress. It allows both the student and the teacher time to make changes in learning activities if it's clear from the assessment that the intended learning is not happening. Pop quizzes are one method of formative assessment that teachers have used for years. Other examples include brief presentations or show-and-tells, exit tickets before leaving a class or a program, or working on KWL (Know, Want to Know, and Learned) activities with youth. Asking teens in a public or school library setting to talk about their learning is a way to include formative assessment activities in programs and services. For example, in a program on wearable technology, teens could demonstrate how they created their technology or show their techniques for attaching LED lights or batteries to their design. In that way, they demonstrate some of the skills learned from the program. Formative assessments are ongoing and can be formal or informal in nature. An example of an informal formative assessment is when a librarian scans the room and uses her knowledge of the students to gauge understanding of the lesson: are students looking confused, tuning out, asking a lot of questions when they should know the answers, and so on.

Summative assessments are used at the end of a program series or a lesson unit. Think of them as the capstone, the unit test, the movie, or the 3-D printed object. Summative assessments are a final evaluation of learning and a final opportunity to reflect on the effectiveness of the learning activity. In the school library, summative assessments are often performed at the end of a unit. For example, a school librarian might work with the history department on a long-term research project. The school librarian and classroom teachers would then co-create the grading rubric and the summative assessment. The school librarian and classroom teachers might then grade the assessment together, divide the projects between them, or grade different components.

Summative assessment in a public library might include a final event to an ongoing program. Using the wearable tech example discussed above, perhaps the teen participants will demonstrate their completed projects to family or friends, sell the projects to benefit the Friends of the Library, or take the final projects to school to showcase with their teachers and peers.

Formative and summative assessments provide richer data. These kinds of assessments allow both the student and teacher, participant and librarian, to gauge ongoing learning and then to determine whether the goals of the unit or program were met. The student can use this knowledge to adjust their work habits, and the librarian should use this knowledge to adjust their instruction and facilitation.

Keep in mind that assessments are meant to examine the outcomes of the lesson or program. It sounds obvious, but it is awfully easy for lessons or programs to drift away from objectives and for the assessments to not align with either. With that in mind, assessments are not the end point of planning. In our experience, the first step to a lesson or program is determining the objectives followed by at least some preliminary plans for an assessment. This helps keep the objectives and the outcomes tightly linked.

# Figure 5-5. Case Study: Providence Public Library's Teen Squad

Employers in Providence, Rhode Island, felt that the area's young adults were not a well-prepared workforce. At least, that's what staff at Providence Public Library were hearing from their youth-serving community partners.[1] Although Providence is home to Brown University, the prestigious Rhode Island School of Design (RISD), and three other universities, it also faces a high poverty rate. In fact, in 2013 Rhode Island had the highest child poverty rate in New England at 21.5%.[2]

Seeking to address this problem, library staff talked to their community partners as well as to the young people who interned, worked, or volunteered at the library to identify what areas of job preparedness were being missed by the school curriculum, and they discovered that it wasn't just technical skills that were lacking: new workforce entrants were also struggling with the "soft skills" needed to be successful in a 21st-century job. In response, the library created the first Teen Squad in 2014.

Originally called the "Teen Tech Squad," "Tech" was dropped from the name as the program evolved to cover a broader range of topics, driven by interests expressed by the library's teenage patrons. The Teen Squad program consists of a series of workshops that take teens through 24 to 30 hours of hands-on connected learning led by professionals and experts from outside the library. Programs have covered the digital humanities and historical interpretation with the Rhode Island Historical Society and the Providence Preservation Society; fashion design with the Rhode Island School of Design; and visual merchandising with staff from the nearby Nordstrom department store. One recent program, "Mind, Body & Selfie," explores, with a local fashion designer, portraiture and identity through the art of selfies.[3] Participants' creative productions are exhibited to their friends, family, and the general public online or in displays at the library.

Teen Services Librarian Shannon Lake says it's easy to see the impact that the Teen Squad has on participants, just by watching the teens grow over the course of the program—not just developing technical skills, but also forming friendships and expressing new interests and curiosity. It's more difficult, she says, to "turn what you see into what you know, on paper."

Providence Public Library uses several measures to assess the performance of a Teen Squad program. Of greatest importance, per Lake, is attendance—but not in the sense of a traditional head count, where number of attendees is the same as magnitude of success. Instead, Lake looks for retention—do teens continue attending and enthusiastically participating in the multi-week sessions? Even more significantly, do teens continue to register for new Teen Squad programs, even if they're unrelated? Some of the teens who attended the program on local history documentation enjoyed it enough that they also signed up for the fashion design class—two very different programs, but they were willing to be open to new opportunities. Similarly, Lake actively tries to find ways to connect students' interest with careers that they might not be aware of—for instance, by scheduling a visual merchandising program with Nordstrom soon after the fashion design program with RISD. Several of the fashion design participants participated in the Nordstrom program to learn about visual merchandising as a fashion-related career option.

The library also looks to partner retention as an indicator of success. If a partner is willing to work with the library on another program, it shows that the communication and collaboration process went well, and that the partner organization also felt that the program was impactful and worth the time and expense. They also value the new audience that their partners bring with them—both teens and adults who may not have been aware of everything the library has to offer beyond books.

Evaluating the "intangibles"—what participants get out of a program—is more difficult. Although Lake gathers plenty of feedback through informal conversations with teens and the partners—along with surveys given to teens at the end of a program and even comments and thank-you notes sent by parents—presenting that mountain of evidence in a meaningful, organized way is still a work in progress for the library. Complicating matters is the fact that the goals for each program vary based on the topic—the outcomes of a video editing workshop may look very different from a tech-lite program that involves turning original fashion designs into miniature dresses.

What's next for outcome assessment for the Teen Squad? Lake hopes to develop a standardized protocol that, along with program-specific assessment, will enable Providence Public Library to identify and evaluate the "commonalities" between the diverse Teen Squad programs.

1. Shannon Lake, personal communication, July 25, 2016.

2. Rhode Island Kids Count, http://www.rikidscount.org/ (accessed February 23, 2017).

3. "Teen Squad: Mind, Body & Selfie," Providence Public Library, http://www.provlib.org/TeenSquadMBS (accessed February 23, 2017).

# Planning Youth Outcomes within a Learning Ecosystem

With methods for evaluation in mind, it's important to focus in on how outcomes and learning relate to each other. Build in time to consider the learning ecosystem in which your participants may be engaged and reflect upon how your outcomes (and associated evaluation methods) may exist within or be reflective of that context. Several possibilities will be highlighted below including:

- Informal Learning and Connected Learning

- Participatory Culture

- Gamification and Badging Systems

## Informal Learning and Connected Learning

Informal learning refers to learning that takes place outside of a formal educational curriculum. This broad definition covers a wide range of experiences—from self-directed projects, to learning that is "incidental" to other activities, to learning that occurs unconsciously through socialization.[13] Informal learning is "lifelong, life-wide, and life-deep."[14] Much, if not most, of the learning that happens in a public library is likely to be informal learning—consider the child who reads every book about dinosaurs or the adult perusing a display about local history.

Connected learning, a concept developed by Mimi Ito and her team at the University of California, Irvine, is an educational framework that emphasizes "connecting" the different contexts and cultures that learners encounter in their everyday lives.[15] The defining elements of connected learning are as follows:

- *Peer Supported:* engages a learner's peer culture, allowing youth to "hang out."

- *Production Centered:* encourages active creations of artifacts that can be shared with others outside of the learning context.

- *Shared Purpose:* allows teens and adults to collaborate and work toward shared goals as partners.

- *Openly Networked:* connects the learner and their activities across contexts (home, school, online, etc.).

- *Academically Oriented* (sometimes called *Opportunity Oriented*): enables youth to develop skills and knowledge that will help them academically or economically, or that enhance their civic participation.

- *Interest Driven:* is driven by the learner's own passions, interests, and motivations.

Not all connected learning is informal. The principles can be incorporated into formal learning—for example, a charter school in New York has based much of its curriculum around connected learning[16] —but the two have much in common and present similar challenges to assessment. Both are influenced by sociocultural approaches to learning, which emphasize that learning occurs in a social and cultural context.[17] Informal and connected learning is more concerned with the behaviors enabled by learning than with the mere acquisition of information.[18] For instance, a successful outcome of a connected learning program about flapper fashion may not be for the learners to be able to remember a list of 1920s fashion trends, but rather for the participants to incorporate flapper design principles when creating their own unique fashion.

Because of the multi-faceted reality of connected learning, outcome based evaluation within this context bares inherent challenges and opportunities. Consider the following:

- *Libraries engage diverse audiences.*

  - *Challenge:* Learners can be more diverse than in a formal setting: in addition to potentially being of different ages, they may come from more diverse backgrounds and have different reasons for visiting or participating in a program.[19] While many classrooms face similar challenges, the teacher can get to know a stable set of participants who (hopefully) share a common goal of graduating at the end of the school year. Informal learning spaces may not have such in-depth knowledge of their visitors.

  - *Opportunity:* Because participants attend programs because of personal interest or passion, libraries are in the unique position of being able to easily capitalize on motivation. Further, the ability to engage diverse audiences add to the richness of the learning environment and the ability to leverage unique individual assets.

- *Libraries provide a variety of (informal) learning experiences.*

  - *Challenge:* These learning experiences can vary greatly from library to library and program to program within a single organization, and even from staff member to staff member. Further, with informal learning, traditional techniques like pre- and post-testing might be impractical or impossible. The formality of surveys and the pass-fail nature of tests may be disruptive to an unstructured learning experience, or even intimidating to a self-directed learner who wasn't anticipating a formal assessment.[20]

  - *Opportunity:* Library staff act as connectors and libraries maintain the flexibility to adapt with community needs and interests. For these reasons, its less important for them to focus on specific content expertise and more of a priority to facilitate with a given audience and within a larger community. This allows participants to be highly involved in a hands-on learning environment and more likely to build 21st century skills like collaboration, creativity, or leadership as secondary outcomes.

# Figure 5-6. Case Study: Digital Artifacts

Many schools use posters to demonstrate knowledge, but then teachers rue the sameness of all the projects. A way to bring participatory culture techniques into this type of project is to shift the project into the digital sphere. By asking students to demonstrate the same knowledge, but in a different media, it's possible to build excitement around traditional work.

At one semi-urban elementary school in the Mid-Atlantic region, there was a shift from paper projects only to including digital media as a presentation option for students in grades three through six. Each year the school has a schoolwide author study. Students select an author to read and create a poster about. The creation of the poster includes a research component, and the assessment used for these projects varies based on the age of the students. Younger students might read only one book and do minimal research about the author, while the oldest and most advanced students might read several books and engage in deeper exploratory research.

The school librarian saw this schoolwide project as an opportunity to teach a myriad of skills, including assessing credibility of sources, providing appropriate credit to content creators, deepening biographical research, and creating a final project. The librarian suggested to teachers that she would teach the skills described above and run an after-school boot camp on a web-based presentation software—Prezi. (So students could use Prezi for their projects instead of creating a poster.) Because the school uses Google Apps for Education, the librarian also taught students how to use Google Slides. The teachers could then focus on other aspects of the author study. From the librarian's perspective, the intended outcomes were increased facility with digital presentations, citation of all sources (including images and video), and increased engagement with an existing project.

In the weeks leading up to the introduction of this project, the librarian made sure to show Prezi to most of the classes, so they would be familiar with the website and the opportunities it offered. The librarian focused lessons around the similarities and differences between Prezi and Google Slides. When the teachers introduced the author study project, the librarian hosted a few after-school sessions helping interested students to create accounts and begin developing their presentation. Students were then able to check in with the library and ask questions throughout the duration of the author study. Students quickly grasped the possibilities of creating a digital presentation. In addition to having a great deal of control and ownership of the final "look" of the author study, students were able to work in multiple media by including videos, hyperlinks, and audio.

While some students still elected to create a traditional poster, many tried a new technology. The adjustment was not only on the part of the student; parents or caregivers were needed to enable the students to use a home computer for the project, to make public library visits, or to allow them to stay after school. Teachers also needed to adjust to evaluating work in a new media. The final product was in a different medium but needed to be held to the same standard using the same rubric. This required some flexibility on the part of the teachers. Outcomes from use of participatory culture techniques in this project were demonstrated by the students who used digital media being very engaged in the project and developing new media skills that they were then eager to share with their peers. For example, as the year went on, the students who created a digital project were frequently the ones to teach their peers skills such as changing a template in Prezi without re-creating the entire project, how to embed video into a Power-Point, and how to cite a photo—all of which demonstrated knowledge gained from using digital tools in the author study project.

- *Connected learning in libraries is inherently social.*

  - *Challenge:* Tests and surveys typically measure the progress of a single individual, but these learning experiences are often highly collaborative and group-oriented.

  - *Opportunity:* Because informal learning spaces are typically group and project oriented, including assessment (particularly formative assessment) and reflection as part of the program implementation process has the capacity to support and enrich learning goals.

## Participatory Culture

Participatory culture is a way of describing a set of literacies and practices that many think are critical to the success of today's children and teens. As the world around us is constantly in flux and new technologies reshape the landscape, children and teens need to learn the skills necessary to navigate a rapidly changing world. Despite the myth of the "digital native" who understands all new technology through osmosis, the truth is that children and teens need education and guidance in using technology, and dispositions and responsibilities for adapting as those technologies shift. Participatory culture takes a generally positive view of this changing world and sees the challenges as opportunities.

Participatory culture is related to informal learning as both include a focus on creativity and content creation, the value of one's personal and cultural experience in creating meaningful learning experiences, and the importance of peer networking and support. Where participatory culture differs from informal learning is in its explicit call to educators to leverage the concepts of participatory culture to reach a new generation of students.[21] Henry Jenkins sets out five criteria for participatory culture:

1. "Low barriers to artistic expression and civic engagement

2. Strong support for creating and sharing one's creations with others

3. Informal mentorship whereby what is known by the most experienced is passed along to novices

4. Members believe that their contributions matter

5. Members feel some degree of social connection with one another (at the least they care what other people think about what they have created)."[22]

Assessing participatory culture is not easy. Because participatory culture emphasizes play, experimentation, collaboration, and peer teaching, it is very challenging to implement and assess in traditional education systems that value quantitative data, individual achievement, and standardized testing. Participatory culture focuses heavily on the process, the community of learning, and the final product. Embedded within participatory culture are practices valued in education, including reflective thinking, self-directed learning, and collaboration.[23] However, these are not easily captured on a multiple-choice test or a quickly designed worksheet. Fostering and then pinpointing outcomes from participatory culture-based learning requires reflective facilitation, flexibility, and careful observation.

The practice of participatory culture should not be considered additional to the teaching and facilitation that a teen library staff member in a school or public library is expected to focus on. Rather, participatory culture represents a shift in *how* ideas are taught and assessed. In this way, participatory culture values the process at least as highly as the outcome. As noted above, mentorship, sharing, and collaboration are cornerstones of participatory culture. These are process-oriented skills, rather than final projects. However, the advocates for participatory culture emphasize that these are skills needed for the 21st-century workforce. Therefore, assessment of a project and program needs to focus as much on the steps youth go through (did they experiment, how did they critically examine their information, did they work collaboratively) as the final product. Possible ways to examine the outcomes for participatory culture include performances (live or digital), portfolios of work, game-based learning, and collaborative projects on real-world problems.

There are significant challenges to implementing these kinds of programs and evaluations in formal and informal learning environments. To begin with, many institutions are still under-resourced in their access to technology. It is hard to collaboratively create a video if the technology required is not present in the institution. Additionally, in the formal school environment, in many instances there is extreme time pressure due to mandates related to curriculum and testing. While acknowledging that participatory culture advocates view this focus as a paradigm shift rather than a new subject, we still have to acknowledge that incorporating this framework can be seen as an additional role and responsibility for library staff. Still, participatory culture is an opportunity for library staff working with teens to infuse their unique skill set into learning.

## Gamification

Gamification refers to "the use of game design elements in non-game contexts,"[24] such as a business that uses a point system to reward em-

## Figure 5-7. Assessment Resources

Andrade, Heidi Goodrich. "Using Rubrics to Promote Thinking and Learning." *Educational Leadership* 57, no. 5 (2000): 13–19.

Donham, Jean. *Enhancing Teaching and Learning: A Leadership Guide for School Library Media Specialists.* New York: Neal-Schuman Publishers, 1998.

Harada, Violet H., and Joan M. Yoshina. *Assessing for Learning: Librarians and Teachers as Partners: Librarians and Teachers as Partners*, 2nd ed., revised and expanded. Santa Barbara, CA: ABC-CLIO, 2010.

Kuhlthau, Carol C., Leslie K. Maniotes, and Ann K. Caspari. *Guided Inquiry: Learning in the 21st Century.* Santa Barbara, CA: ABC-CLIO, 2015.

Vance, Anita L., and Robbie Nickel, eds. *Assessing Student Learning in the School Library Media Center.* Chicago: American Library Association, 2007.

Wallace, Virginia L., and Whitney Norwood Husid. *Collaborating for Inquiry-Based Learning: School Librarians and Teachers Partner for Student Achievement.* Santa Barbara, CA: ABC-CLIO, 2011.

ployees who answer questions on a business's intranet, or a fitness tracker that allows friends to compete to take the most steps on a given day. Unlike simple "play" or "fun," the concept of a "game" involves structure, rules, and at least some amount of effort or difficulty. Gamification is generally intended to encourage desired behaviors or completion of certain tasks—when implemented properly, it is both motivating and engaging.

Gamification can be a valuable tool for implementing outcome-based assessment techniques. Since games generally center around "winning" or completing the game successfully, often after mastering an increasingly difficult series of tasks,[25] they provide a natural way to gauge a learner's progress.[26] Games and gamification have the added benefit of offering transparent success and failure to the player: with a well-designed experience, players can tell how well they are performing or even compare their progress to others without needing any type of answer key.

Gamification elements can also be quite useful for evaluating the success of a library program or initiative, providing motivation to participants to self-report activity that might otherwise only be measurable with efforts like surveys or interviews. Gamification can also be used to gather data from patrons—interests and hobbies listed in online profiles, for instance—that would not normally be as easy to collect. Location check-ins, rewarded with badges or points, can help assess engagement by unobtrusively tracking repeat visits.[27]

Badging is a popular tool used in gamification. Just like Boy Scout Merit Badges, digital badges are social markers of expertise, achievement, or interest.[28] A unique strength of online gamification is that it can easily capture activities that occur outside of the library (a key component of connected learning, covered earlier in this chapter). For example, when Pierce County (Washington) Public Library developed their Teen Summer Challenge, the staff wanted to expand beyond simply encouraging and tracking reading. With the goal of inspiring teens to participate in STEAM (science, technology, engineering, arts, and math) activities, while getting involved with the local community, they designed a set of badges relating to both online and offline activities encouraging teens to "play, discover, and learn."[29] With the help of the digital badging system, the library was able to track how many participants completed activities like volunteering at animal shelters or going for a hike.[30] This was a way to determine if outcomes were met even if teens did not participate in library activities in an actual library building.

# Conclusion

Outcome-based evaluation is increasingly popular in libraries, and knowing the fundamentals of the what, why, and how of evaluation in general and OBE more specifically will help you better understand how your programs and services are supporting and meeting the needs of teen library users. Done well, OBE can help you improve your own instruction and facilitation skills. Developing your skills in OBE will prove useful in multiple arenas. Outcome-based evaluation can help you demonstrate the effectiveness of your programs to a wider audience—whether they are your supervisor, board, funders, or government agencies—and should be a part of every librarian's skill set.

# Notes

1. Benjamin Herold, "Technology in Education: An Overview," *Education Week*, February 5, 2016, http://www.edweek.org/ew/issues/technology-in-education/ (accessed February 23, 2017).

2. Partnership for 21st Century Learning, "Framework for 21st Century Learning," http://www.p21.org/our-work/p21-framework (accessed February 23, 2017).

3. Linda W. Braun, Maureen Hartman, Sandra Hughes-Hassell, and Kafi Kumasi, *The Future of Library Services for and with Teens: A Call to Action* (IMLS and YALSA, January 2014), http://www.ala.org/yaforum/sites/ala.org.yaforum/files/content/YALSA_nationalforum_final.pdf (accessed February 21, 2017).

4. William G. Spady, *Outcome-Based Education: Critical Issues and Answers* (Arlington, VA: American Association of School Administrators, 1994). 2.

5. "Outcome Based Evaluation Basics," Institute of Museum and Library Services, https://www.imls.gov/grants/outcome-based-evaluation/basics (accessed February 23, 2017).

6. Lietzau Zeth, Keith Curry Lance, Amanda Rybin, and Carla Molliconi, preface to *Public Libraries, a Wise Investment: A Return on Investment Study of Colorado Libraries*, by Nicolle Steffen (Denver: Library Research Service, 2009).

7. New York State Education Department, "NYS Library Development: Outcome-Based Evaluation—Basic OBE Training Manual," Slide 6 of 57, NYSED. gov, http://www.nysl.nysed.gov/libdev/obe/basic/sld006.htm (accessed February 23, 2017).

8. Philip M. Turner and Ann Marlow Riedling, *Helping Teachers Teach: A School Library Media Specialist's Role* (Westport, CT: Libraries Unlimited, 2003).

9. New York State Education Department, NYS Library Development, "Outcome-Based Evaluation—Basic OBE Training Manual, Outcomes Data Sources Tip Sheet," NYSED.gov, http://www.nysl.nysed.gov/libdev/obe/basic/ods_tip.htm (accessed February 23, 2017).

10. Alicia Wilson-Ahlstrom, Nicole Yohalem, David DuBois, Peter Ji, and Barbara Hillaker, *From Soft Skills to Hard Data: Measuring Youth Program Outcomes*, 2nd ed. (Forum for Youth Investment, January 2014), http://forumfyi.org/files/soft_skills_hard_data_single.pdf (accessed February 23, 2017).

11. Sarah Anne Murphy, "How Data Visualization Supports Academic Library Assessment," *College & Research Libraries News*, October 1, 2015, http://crln.acrl.org/content/76/9/482.full (accessed February 23, 2017).

12. "Use the Best Information about What Works," Ready by 21, August 31, 2011, http://www.readyby21.org/toolkits/use-best-information-about-what-works (accessed February 23, 2017).

13. Daniel Schugurensk, "The Forms of Informal Learning: Towards a Conceptualization of the Field," Wall Working Paper, no. 19 (2000), https://tspace.library.utoronto.ca/bitstream/1807/2733/2/19formsofinformal.pdf (accessed February 23, 2017).

14. Kalie Sacco, John H. Falk, and James Bell, "Informal Science Education: Lifelong, Life-Wide, Life-Deep," *PLoS Biology* 12, no. 11 (2014), doi:10.1371/journal.pbio.1001986.

15. Mizuko Ito, Kris Gutiérrez, Sonia Livingstone, Bill Penuel, Jean Rhodes, Katie Salen, Juliet Schor, Julian Sefton-Green, and S. Craig Watkins, *Connected Learning: An Agenda for Research and Design* (Digital Media and Learning Research Hub, January 2013), http://dmlhub.net/wp-content/uploads/files/Connected_Learning_report.pdf (accessed February 22, 2017).

16. Christo Sims, "Boss Level at Quest to Learn: Connected Learning in a Public School," National Writing Project, Digital IS, 2013, http://digitalis.nwp.org/boss-level-at-quest-to-learn-connected-learning-in-a-public-school (accessed February 23, 2017).

17. Jean Lave and Etienne Wenger, *Situated Learning: Legitimate Peripheral Participation* (Cambridge: Cambridge University Press, 1998); Mizuko Ito et al., *Hanging Out, Messing Around, and Geeking Out* (Cambridge, MA: MIT Press, 2013).

18. Vera Michalchik and Lawrence Gallagher, "Naturalizing Assessment," *Curator: The Museum Journal* 53, no. 2 (2010): 209–19, doi:10.1111/j.2151-6952.2010.00020.x.

19. Michalchik and Gallagher, "Naturalizing Assessment."

20. Ibid.; Bell, *Learning Science in Informal Environments*.

21. Richard T. Hudson, Sean Duncan, and Carlton Reeve, *Affinity Spaces for Informal Science Learning: Developing a Research Agenda* (2016), p. 38, http://www.informalscience.org/sites/default/files/AffinitySpacesFinalReport.pdf, (accessed February 23, 2017).

22. Henry Jenkins, *Confronting the Challenges of Participatory Culture: Media Education for the 21st Century* (Cambridge, MA: MIT Press, 2009), 7.

23. Ibid., 56.

24. Sebastian Deterding, Dan Dixon, Rilla Khaled, and Lennart Nacke, "From

Game Design Elements to Gamefulness: Defining Gamification," in *Envisioning Future Media Environments*, 9–15, Proceedings of 15th International Academic MindTrek Conference, Finland, Tampare, doi:0.1145/2181037.2181040.

25. James Paul Gee, "What Video Games Have to Teach Us about Literacy and Learning," *Computers in Entertainment* 1, no. 1 (2003): 20, doi:10.1145/950566.950595.

26. Katie Salen, *Quest to Learn: Developing the School for Digital Kids* (Cambridge, MA: MIT Press, 2011).

27. Sara Ryan, "Tell the Story: Use Outcomes to Show the Difference Your Program Makes," *Young Adult Library Services (YALS)* 12, no. 1 (Fall 2013): 13–15.

28. Katie Davis and Simrat Singh, "Digital Badges in Afterschool Learning: Documenting the Perspectives and Experiences of Students and Educators," *Computers & Education* 88 (2015): 72–83, doi:10.1016/j.compedu.2015.04.011.

29. Elise Doney, "Taking the Teen Summer Challenge to New Heights, Pierce County Style," *School Library Journal*, September 2, 2014, http://www.slj.com/2014/09/programs/taking-the-teen-summer-challenge-to-new-heights-pierce-county-style/ (accessed February 23, 2017).

30. "Teen Summer Challenges," Pierce County Library Teens, https://www.pierce-countylibrary.org/kids-teens/summer-reading-2012/teens.htm (accessed February 23, 2017).

# APPENDIX A

# The Future of Library Services for and with Teens: A Call to Action

## EXECUTIVE SUMMARY

Libraries provide a lifeline for teens, their families and communities across the nation by providing a safe and supervised space for adolescents to engage in creative, educational activities with caring adults and mentors. But a variety of significant developments point to a need for libraries to change in order to successfully meet the needs of today's teens.

*The Future of Library Services for and with Teens: a Call to Action*, is the result of a yearlong national forum conducted by the Young Adult Library Services Association (YALSA) in 2013, with funding provided by the Institute of Museum and Library services. The *Call to Action* lays out a new path for serving 21st century teens through libraries. This 2014 report shows that many libraries are continuing to grapple with diminishing resources while at the same time struggling to meet the needs of a changing teen population. Additionally, significant developments in technology have led to the need to rethink how services for and with teens are best created and delivered. The *Call to Action* provides recommendations on how libraries must address challenges and re-envision their teen services in order to meet the needs of their individual communities and to collectively ensure that the nation's 40+ million teens develop the skills they need to be productive citizens.

# The Issues

### Teens Make Up a Significant Portion of Library Users

There are over 40 million adolescents, aged 12–17, living in the United States today, and they use libraries. A 2013 Pew survey found that 72% of 16- to 17-year-olds had used a public library in 2012.

### Library Services and Resources for Teens Are in Jeopardy

Library closures, reduced hours, lack of staff, and insufficient resources mean that teens in many communities no longer have access to the resources, knowledge, and services they need to support their academic, emotional, and social development, to master 21st-century skills, and to ensure that they become productive citizens.

### There Has Been a Significant Shift in the Demographics of Teens

According to an analysis of the 2010 census data completed by the Annie E. Casey Foundation, there are currently 74.2 million children under the age of eighteen in the United States; 46% of them are children of color. Additionally, more than one-fifth of America's children are immigrants or children of immigrants. Now is the time for the field of librarianship, the population of which is overwhelmingly Caucasian, to consider what these demographic changes mean to school and public library services and programs for and with teens.

### Technology Continues to Impact Communication Methods, Teaching, and Learning

Teens' use of technology (smart phones, tablets, laptops, the Internet, etc.) is pervasive. However, ownership of technology devices continues to vary across socioeconomic and racial demographics. Now is the time for public and school libraries to systematically determine how technology will affect the future of library services for and with teens, with special attention to the access gaps that continue to exist.

### Teens Are Entering the Workforce without Critical Skills

In the last three decades, the skills required for young adults to succeed in the workforce have changed drastically, but the skills emphasized in schools have not kept up with these changes. Libraries need to create the kind of spaces, services, and opportunities that today's teens need in order to succeed in school and in life.

## The Paradigm Shift and Libraries

Several important factors have come together in such a way that libraries are experiencing a seismic shift. Ever since computers entered library spaces, public and school libraries have been on a precipice of change. The library can no longer be viewed as a quiet place to connect to physical content. Instead it needs to evolve into a place, physical and virtual, where individuals can learn how to connect and use all types of resources, from physical books to apps to experts in a local, regional, or national community. Libraries must leverage new technologies and become kitchens for "mixing resources" in order to empower teens to build skills, develop understanding, create and share, and overcome adversity. In addition to the impact of new technologies, the definition of literacy has expanded beyond the cognitive ability to read and write, to a recognition that literacy is a social act that involves basic modes of participating in the world. New research also points to a concept of connected learning, in which studies show that young people learn best when that learning is connected to their passions, desires, and interests.

## What Teens Need from Libraries

**Bridge the growing digital and knowledge divide:** School and public libraries must ensure that in addition to providing access to digital tools, that they also provide formal and informal opportunities for teens to learn to use them in meaningful and authentic ways.

**Leverage Teens' Motivation to Learn:** Too often teens' desire to learn is thwarted by an educational system too focused on testing, unwilling to adopt culturally relevant pedagogy, or so strapped for funding that only basic resources are available. Libraries live outside of a school's formal academic achievement sphere and offer a space where interest based learning can occur in a risk-free environment. Public and school libraries, therefore, need to embrace their role as both formal and informal learning spaces.

**Provide Workforce Development Training:** In order to address the growing need for a skilled workforce, school and public libraries have the responsibility to enable teens to learn in relevant, real world 21st century contexts.

**Serve as the Connector between Teens and other Community Agencies:** Libraries are only one of many organizations with a vision to build better futures for teens. Too often, however, teens are unaware of the services offered in their communities. As many of today's teens are faced with serious social and economic challenges, libraries must provide teens the assistance they need.

# Implications for Libraries

In order to meet the needs of today's teens and to continue to provide value to their communities, libraries need to revisit their fundamental structure, including these components:

**Audience:** the focus is on serving all teens in the community, not just those who are regular users of the physical library space

**Collections:** are tailored to meet the unique needs of the teens in the particular community they serve, and are expanded to include digital resources as well as experts and mentors

**Space:** a flexible physical library space that allows for teens to work on a variety of projects with each other and adult mentors to create and share content. Virtual spaces also allow for teens to connect with each other and with experts. Libraries recognize that teens need and want to make use of the entire library space or site, not just a designated teen area.

**Programming:** programs occur year-round, leverage the unique attributes of libraries, allow for teens to gain skills through exploration of their interests and measure outcomes in terms of knowledge gained or skills learned.

**Staffing:** Degreed library professionals focus on developing and managing teen services at the programmatic level, while face-to-face encounters are made up of a hybrid of staff and skilled volunteers who act as mentors, coaches, and connectors

**Youth participation:** is integrated throughout the teen services program and enables teens to provide both on-the-fly and structured feedback for the library staff. Teen participation is not limited to formally organized groups

**Outreach:** is on-going and occurs in order to identify the needs of teens in the community and then work with partners to alleviate those needs.

**Policy:** focuses on serving teens no matter where they are. The policies are flexible and easy to update in order to reflect changing needs

**Professional development:** Takes a whole library/whole school approach to planning, delivering and evaluating teen services. Investigates attributes and resources unique to libraries and identifies means for leveraging those to achieve library goals.

Today's 40+ million adolescents face an increasing array of social issues, barriers, and challenges that many of them are unable to overcome on their own. With nearly 7,000 teens dropping out of high school per day, and approximately 40% of high school graduates not proficient in traditional literacy skills, the nation is in danger of losing an entire generation, which in turn will lead to a shortage of skilled workers and engaged citizens. Now is the time for public and school libraries to join with other key stakeholders and take action to help solve the issues and problems that negatively impact teens, and ultimately the future of the nation. These challenges are not insurmountable. It is a moral imperative for libraries to leverage their skills and resources to effect positive change and better the lives of millions of teens. In turn, libraries will be providing an invaluable service to their community and position themselves as an indispensable community resource.

# Teens First Infographic

## REIMAGINED LIBRARY SERVICES FOR AND WITH TEENS

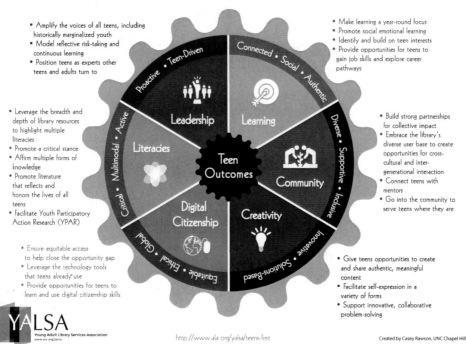

- Amplify the voices of all teens, including historically marginalized youth
- Model reflective risk-taking and continuous learning
- Position teens as experts other teens and adults turn to

- Make learning a year-round focus
- Promote social emotional learning
- Identify and build on teen interests
- Provide opportunities for teens to gain job skills and explore career pathways

- Leverage the breadth and depth of library resources to highlight multiple literacies
- Promote a critical stance
- Affirm multiple forms of knowledge
- Promote literature that reflects and honors the lives of all teens
- Facilitate Youth Participatory Action Research (YPAR)

- Build strong partnerships for collective impact
- Embrace the library's diverse user base to create opportunities for cross-cultural and inter-generational interaction
- Connect teens with mentors
- Go into the community to serve teens where they are

- Ensure equitable access to help close the opportunity gap
- Leverage the technology tools that teens already use
- Provide opportunities for teens to learn and use digital citizenship skills

- Give teens opportunities to create and share authentic, meaningful content
- Facilitate self-expression in a variety of forms
- Support innovative, collaborative problem-solving

**YALSA**
Young Adult Library Services Association
www.ala.org/yalsa

http://www.ala.org/yalsa/teens-first

Created by Casey Rawson, UNC Chapel Hill

# Core Professional Values for the Teen Services Profession

## Foreword

These core values were developed in 2013-2014 by the Professional Values Task Force of the Young Adult Library Services Association (YALSA). Members of the task force were Sarah Debraski, Meg Finney, Gretchen Kolderup, Amanda Murphy, Lalitha Nataraj (chair) and Vivian Wynn. YALSA's Board of Directors adopted the guidelines on June 27, 2015.

## About YALSA

The mission of the Young Adult Library Services Association (YALSA) is to support library staff in alleviating the challenges teens face, and in putting all teens—especially those with the greatest needs—on the path to successful and fulfilling lives. YALSA is a subspecialty of the American Library Association, the world's largest and oldest library organization, and a financially stable 501(c)3 not-for-profit.

To learn more about YALSA or to access other national guidelines relating to library services for and with teens, go to www.ala.org/yalsa.

## Introduction

This document includes **nine core values** that define professionalism for those who work for and with teens through libraries. Additionally, for those who work for and with teens through libraries. Additionally, this document provides examples of sample indicators for practices that resonate with each value. Potential users of this tool include library administrators, teen services library staff, and faculty at graduate schools of library and information science. The tool is not intended to provide a measure of the skills and knowledge that an individual must have in order to be successful in teen services; rather, the *Core Professional Values* are viewed as fundamental underlying principles that guide the decisions, actions, and behaviors of library staff working with and for teens. The *Core Professional Values* complements the American Library Association's *Code of Ethics*: the Code outlines a broad moral standard for individuals working in libraries, whereas the YALSA values provides further context for those who work for and with teens. "Professionalism in Physical Therapy: Core Values" was consulted when developing this document.

| Core Values... | Value is... | A person practicing this value... |
| --- | --- | --- |
| Accountability | Active acceptance of the responsibility for the diverse roles, obligations and actions of the job, including self-regulation and other behaviors that positively influence teens, the profession and the community | • Responds to teen needs<br><br>• Seeks and responds to feedback from multiple sources<br><br>• Acknowledges and accepts the consequences of one's actions<br><br>• Adheres to codes of ethics, standards of practice and other policies that govern the profession, including those created by ALA and YALSA<br><br>• Communicates regularly with others about work-related actions<br><br>• Strives for continuous improvement<br><br>• Maintains membership in professional organizations |

| Core Values... | Value is... | A person practicing this value... |
|---|---|---|
| Collaboration | Fosters relationships within the library and within the community in order to best serve teens | • Works with other departments within the organization to create a holistic approach to serving teens<br><br>• Fosters partnerships with schools and other community organizations that serve youth<br><br>• Leverages the talent, expertise, and resources available in the community |
| Compassion | Strives to identify with others' experiences. Shows concern, empathy, and consideration for the needs and values of others | • Communicates effectively, both verbally and non-verbally, with others, taking into consideration individual differences in learning styles, language, cognitive abilities, etc.<br><br>• Builds and maintains knowledge of teens' social, emotional, mental, and physical development and how they shape the teen experience<br><br>• Strives to understand teens' lives from their perspective in order to create genuine connections<br><br>• Places the needs of teens above one's own<br><br>• Provides services for and with underserved and underrepresented teen populations |

| Core Values... | Value is... | A person practicing this value... |
|---|---|---|
| Excellence | Consistently uses current knowledge and theory while understanding personal limits. Integrates judgment and the teen perspective. Embraces advancement, challenges mediocrity, and works toward development of new knowledge | • Demonstrates investment in the profession<br><br>• Participates in collaborative practices to promote high quality outcomes<br><br>• Demonstrates high levels of knowledge and skill in all aspects of teen services<br><br>• Engages in acquisition of new knowledge throughout one's career<br><br>• Shares knowledge with others<br><br>• Demonstrates emotional intelligence and processes emotional information to navigate the social environment<br><br>• Demonstrates mastery of soft skills including social norms, communication, language, personal habits, interpersonal skills, supervising people, leadership, etc. to ensure successful interactions with a range of stakeholders, including supervisors, teens, and community partners<br><br>• Projects a professional image, including suitable appearance/dress, use of correct manners and etiquette, effective communication, and appropriate personal behavior. Recognizes that different situations can call for different dress, behaviors, speech, etiquette, etc. |

| Core Values... | Value is... | A person practicing this value... |
|---|---|---|
| Inclusion | Recognizes and respects the wide variety in people's heritages and lived experiences | • Builds knowledge in order to understand the backgrounds and lived experiences of those in the community the library serves, especially when they differ from one's own<br><br>• Respects and fosters a diversity of viewpoints<br><br>• Recognizes and refrains from acting on one's social, cultural, gender, and sexual biases<br><br>• Confronts harassment and bias among one's self and others<br><br>• Welcomes, values and creates a safe environment for and with teens of all cultural and socio-economic backgrounds and those with different abilities and identities<br><br>• Includes teens in library decision-making<br><br>• Creates meaningful, skill-building volunteer and leadership opportunities for and with teens<br><br>• Recognizes teen expertise and creates ways for that expertise to be shared |

| Core Values... | Value is... | A person practicing this value... |
|---|---|---|
| Innovation | Approaches projects and challenges with a creative, innovative mindset | • Develops, tests and evaluates new ideas<br><br>• Pushes the boundaries of what the library is and what it does for and with teens<br><br>• Maximizes resources to provide the best library services and experiences for and with teens<br><br>• Recognizes that learning comes from failure and experimentation<br><br>• Demonstrates a willingness to take calculated risks to improve teen services |

| Core Values... | Value is... | A person practicing this value... |
|---|---|---|
| Integrity | Upholds strong moral and ethical principles. Acts truthfully, fairly, and without ulterior motive | • Puts patrons/library above personal interest or gain<br><br>• Maintains confidentiality<br><br>• Adheres to the highest standards of the profession, including those articulated by ALA and YALSA<br><br>• Articulates and internalizes stated ideals and professional values<br><br>• Resolves dilemmas with respect to a consistent set of core values<br><br>• Is trustworthy<br><br>• Takes responsibility to be an integral part of the library and community<br><br>• Chooses employment situations that are congruent with the profession's values and ethical standards<br><br>• Acts on the basis of professional values even when the results of the behavior may place one's self at risk |
| Professional Duty | Committed to meeting one's professional obligations, to serving the profession and to positively influence the community | • Pursues continuing education opportunities regularly<br><br>• Keeps abreast of teen issues and library trends<br><br>• Contributes to the library community and supports the growth of other librarians and library workers<br><br>• Promotes the profession |

| Core Values... | Value is... | A person practicing this value... |
|---|---|---|
| Social Responsibility | Promotes the mutual trust between the profession and the larger public. Responds to societal needs as they relate to teens and libraries | • Can articulate the teen perspective when friction arises between adults (patrons or staff) and teens in the library<br><br>• Seeks opportunities both inside and outside the library to speak up and act for teen services rather than waiting to be asked to do so<br><br>• Advocates for the educational, developmental, and recreational needs of teens, especially as they relate to library services<br><br>• Promotes policies that support the needs and interest of teens and their families<br><br>• Advocates for changes in laws, regulations, standards, and guidelines that affect the ability of libraries to deliver excellent library services for and with teens<br><br>• Promotes community volunteerism<br><br>• Provides leadership in the community<br><br>• Participates in collaborative relationships with other youth service providers and the public at large<br><br>• Ensures the blending of social justice and economic efficiency of services |

# About the Authors and Editors

## Editors

### Linda W. Braun

Linda W Braun is a YALSA past president, the YALSA CE consultant, and a learning consultant at LEO: Librarians & Educators Online. She is a coauthor of *The Future of Library Services for and with Teens: A Call to Action.*

### Shannon Peterson

Shannon Peterson is the Youth Services manager at Kitsap Regional Library and coordinates systemwide initiatives related to early learning, STEM, and college and career readiness. Shannon is a past president of the Young Adult Library Services Association (YALSA) as well as a recipient of the Washington State Library Association's Visionary Service to Youth Award.

## Authors

### Megan Christine-Carlin Burton

Megan is a Teen Services librarian at the Kitsap Regional Library in Bremerton, Washington. She is committed to designing for and with young people in active learning spaces that celebrate diversity, digital media, and most importantly youth voice. In 2015 she was named one of the finalists for the 21st Century Award from the University of Washington iSchool and was the recipient of the Jeannette M. Privat Endowment for Librarianship.

## Maureen Hartman

Maureen L. Hartman is a former YALSA board member, public library leader, and coauthor of *The Future of Library Services for and with Teens: A Call to Action*. She is currently the division manager for Strategic Services for the Hennepin County Library in Minnesota.

## Kelly Hoffman

Kelly M. Hoffman is a PhD candidate at the University of Maryland's iSchool, where she is researching connected learning in public libraries and political information sharing.

## Crystle Martin

Crystle Martin is a postdoctoral researcher at the Digital Media and Learning Hub. She holds a PhD in Education with a specialization in Digital Media and MLIS. She studies youth interest-driven learning and how libraries can create equitable opportunities learning. Crystle is currently the editor of YALSA's official journal, *YALS*, and is secretary for the YALSA Board of Directors.

## Juan Rubio

Juan Rubio designs, develops, and manages educational technology programs with digital media, such as games, interactive storytelling, and augmented reality narratives. He is the Digital Media and Learning program manager for the Seattle Public Library. Juan has a master's degree in Media Studies from the New School University in New York City and studied TV and Film at Howard University School of Communications in Washington DC. Originally from Honduras, he is fluent in Spanish.

## Jessi Snow

Jess Snow is the Teen Services Team Leader of Teen Central of the Boston Public Library. She is a YALSA Board of Directors member 2016–17 and a regular *YALSAblog* blogger on outreach to underserved and underrepresented populations provided by staff in teen services. Outreach is one of her priority areas for Boston's teen services.

## Natalie Green Taylor

Natalie Greene Taylor, PhD, is an assistant professor at the University of South Florida. Her research focuses on young people's access to information. More specifically, she studies youth information behavior, information intermediaries, and information policy as it affects youth information access. She is an associate editor of *Library Quarterly*, has coauthored two books—*Digital Literacy and Digital Inclusion: Information Policy and the Public Library and Libraries, Human Rights, and Social Justice: Enabling Access and Promoting Inclusion*—and co-edited the book *Perspectives on Libraries as Institutions of Human Rights and Social Justice.*

## Amanda Waugh

Amanda Waugh is a doctoral candidate in the iSchool at the University of Maryland College Park and a former school librarian. Her research interests are focused on youth in online communities as well as the impact school libraries have on their school communities.

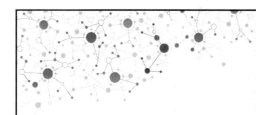